VICTORIAN BUILDINGS IN BRISTOL

BY CLARE CRICK

£1·40

Foreword

We have enjoyed Georgian Bristol to the point of ignoring the city's Victorian buildings. But Bristol's Victorian architecture has enormous variety and character. Quality abounds in the original work of several local architects, such as Foster and Wood, Gingell, and Oatley. There are many outstanding buildings by visiting architects, such as Street, Waterhouse and Sedding. Cockerell, Butterfield and Holden did some of their earliest important work in Bristol and E. W. Godwin, who was undoubtedly one of the finest Victorian architects, was born, raised and in practice in Bristol before moving to London.

This booklet sets out to track a path through the complex maze of Bristol's Victorian architecture. It is not a guide book but it will surely be indispensable to every subsequent writer of local guides and town trails. Many of the buildings, which are discussed and illustrated, have long since disappeared. But this visual reconstruction is vital if we are to recreate the pattern of Bristol's architecture, to trace the high points of quality and influence, to determine the individuality of our local architects, and, above all, to value accurately the buildings that remain. It is not suggested that all buildings of age have architectural merit and care should be taken to distinguish between those of real merit which should be preserved and those which are of marginal worth only.

It will be noted that several of the architects' drawings and many of the engraved views illustrated here, come from the collection of the City Art Gallery where the author is the Assistant Curator of Fine Art. The Museum and Art Gallery are the principal trustees of our heritage but much use has also been made of material in the care of other local institutions and private companies for whose kind and always generous help we are extremely grateful.

Andrew Breach, C.B.E., F.C.I.S., F.B.S., J.P.,
Chairman, Bristol and West Building Society

REGENCY AND EARLY VICTORIAN ARCHITECTURE

In 1823 Sir Robert Smirke began designs for his masterpiece, the British Museum. In the same year his scheme for the rebuilding of Bristol's Council House and the widening of Corn Street was approved. The employment of outside architects in Bristol was relatively novel and the work of Smirke and Charles Robert Cockerell represents a significant change in both architectural styles and practice.

Until the Napoleonic Wars had ended most of the architects were local residents of Bristol or Bath. Their work and the many major buildings by anonymous builders and master masons were loosely bound to the rules of Roman classicism and were familiar in the city, on the slopes of Kingsdown, over Clifton and in the suburbs of Montpelier and St. Pauls. These buildings were confident, elegant and friendly.

But by 1800 local architectural enterprise and craftsmanship had begun to falter, primarily for economic reasons. Balanced against the heroic conception of covering Clifton with terraces and crescents in imitation of Bath was a sorry story of decline and ill-starred speculation. It is significant that the proposals for a new Council House had been on the shelf for over thirty years.

The end of the war saw an increase in building activity and the appearance of the Greek Revival style in Bristol. Both Smirke and Cockerell had visited not only Italy but also Greece. Scholarly publications based on careful observation and archaeological study of the antiquities of ancient Greece had appeared in the latter years of the 18th century and were exemplified in Britain by James Stuart's and Nicholas Revitt's, *Antiquities of Athens*, published between 1762 and 1794. A new fashion emerged demanding a purer classical architecture based on original evidence rather than on second-hand Roman or Renaissance interpretations. Sir Robert Smirke's (1780–1867) Council House was completed in 1827 (see Plate 1). It is grave, sparingly decorated and very precisely composed. The facade was flatteringly set at a shallow oblique angle to Corn Street allowing the giant Ionic columns their full effect. The corner site of Corn and Broad Streets further enhances the rectangular plan which, with its concentration on geometrical form, Smirke considered to be a vital component of modern functional design.

Smirke is further represented in Bristol by the Church of St. George on Brandon Hill of 1823. It compares closely with the architect's London churches. But in Bristol its proud Doric portico and small cupola were used to more romantic effect against an open and then unencumbered hillside overlooking the city.

When the occasion arose for the building of premises for the recently founded Bristol Philosophical and Literary Institution, a professional London architect was chosen, once again superseding the local building masons. A site was purchased at the bottom of Park Street, the steep Georgian-built concourse which provided the main thoroughfare between Bristol and Clifton. The building was opened in 1823 and is the one which we know today as the Freemasons' Hall. It was designed early in the career of Charles Robert Cockerell (1788–1863), who had initally made his name as an archaeologist after being associated with some spectacular excavations in Greece and Turkey. His passion for classical antiquities was later to be combined with an admiration for the works of Sir Christopher Wren which prompted his development of a more flexible and inventive style than the dictates of the Greek Revival generally allowed.

The lecture room, galleries and library housed in the Institution were to occupy a very steep street corner which prevented the use of a symmetrical facade design and a tall circular Greek portico was therefore placed at the corner of the building.

In 1829 a church at Hotwells, funded by public subscription, was built to meet the needs of the Spa community which had been established there in the late 18th century. Cockerell's design for the Church of Holy Trinity (see Plate 2), offered a centralised plan, its main feature on the southern entrance being a giant coffered niche below a broken pediment decorated with a dove descending in a glory of rays. The virtuosity of this design was carried into the interior, which was comprised of Tuscan columns, a saucer-shaped dome and galleries, all unfortunately gutted during the Second World War.

Cockerell's association with Bristol was to continue through his successful career. In 1844 as architect to the Bank of England he was commissioned to design branch banks at Plymouth, Manchester, Liverpool and Bristol. All were similar in plan and elevation, consisting of a pediment crowning an attic storey and of an order attached to the lower storey. In Bristol's branch in Broad Street (see Plate 3), an imposing Doric order was chosen and, although the building occupied a narrow street frontage, the introduction of two entrance porches and the use of projecting piers gave visual distinction to this monumental design, which, on its completion, must have provided a dominating metropolitan presence in the old financial quarter.

Many more modest examples of the Greek Revival can still be seen. A terrace in Great George Street displays an Ionic colonnade of single and coupled columns. From Small Street in the old quarter one can pass through a barely noticeable segmental-headed entrance bearing honeysuckle ornament to a courtyard serving stucco-faced office buildings known as Albion Chambers. Eighteenth century buildings on the north side of Queen Square had been destroyed during the Reform Riots of 1831 and rebuilding over the following five years tentatively incorporated Greek elements into a terrace design, the divisional pilasters being interrupted by a range of cast-iron balconies.

By the 1830's accomplished local architects could provide Bristol with impressive public buildings and churches which reveal a confident and often inventive handling of current architectural styles.

A local architect, James Foster, a former assistant to the eminent Bristol architect, William Paty, was to construct a double arcade off Broadmead, the lower portion of which survives today. Ionic columns flank each entrance and mark divisions between the bay-windowed shop fronts. These glass-roofed passages were six hundred feet long and rivalled comparable arcades in Cheltenham, Bath and London.

In 1836 the Bristol General Cemetery Company was formed to meet the urgent need for an increase of burial grounds. Land at Arno's Vale within a mile of the centre was purchased, laid out as a cemetery and consecrated in 1840. Here designs by the Bristol architect, Charles Underwood, were followed in the construction of two Greek Doric lodges (see Plate 4), and two chapels. Of the latter one displayed a simple Ionic portico and the other was of a later, more elaborate design. These served members of the Established and Dissenting Churches separately. The Vale afforded an unusual opportunity for a picturesque fusion of classical architecture and a natural park-like setting.

Charles Dyer (1794–1848) was the son of a Bristol surgeon and trained under William Brooks, the London architect.

PLATE 1

The Council House, Corn Street
Sir Robert Smirke, 1822–7
Line engraving.   *City Art Gallery, Bristol*

The Church of Holy Trinity, Hotwell Road
Charles Robert Cockerell, 1829–30.
Line engraving.   *City Art Gallery, Bristol*

PLATE 2

PLATE 3

The former Bristol Branch of the Bank of England, Broad Street
Charles Robert Cockerell 1844–47.

National Monuments Record

PLATE 4

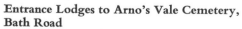

Entrance Lodges to Arno's Vale Cemetery, Bath Road
Charles Underwood, 1837–40.
Avon Branch of the R.I.B.A., Bristol Society of Architects

PLATE 5

**The Victoria Rooms,
Queen's Road**
Charles Dyer, 1839–41.
In about 1911 the sphinxes
were removed and the
forecourt redesigned by
Edwin Rickards to display
an ornamental Baroque
fountain and a statue of
Edward VII.
Lithograph.
City Art Gallery, Bristol

PLATE 6

**Roman Catholic Pro-Cathedral,
Park Place, Clifton**
Watercolour design by Henry Edmund
Goodridge. Circa 1834. Work on this
building was abandoned in 1845,
leaving only the basement storey
intact. A temporary superstructure was
added by Charles Hansom, enabling
the Church of the Apostles to open in
1848. For the third stage of building,
1870–6, by Hansom, see Plate 29.
National Monuments Record

Dyer was to be much employed as a designer of churches and institutional buildings in his native city. He is chiefly remembered for the spectacular Victoria Rooms (see Plate 5), designs for which were first exhibited at the Royal Academy in 1832. The Assembly Rooms in the Mall at Clifton could no longer accommodate the expanding fashionable population of this residential area and it was a Conservative body which advanced proposals for a new concert hall and meeting rooms. Dyer's monumental Corinthian building has a giant portico of eight columns and a rich entablature and pediment decorated with Jabez Tyleys's sculptural representation of Minerva in a chariot being driven by Apollo and preceded by the Hours and Graces. The effect was more ambitious in conception than any other neo-Grecian building in Bristol. The seventy-one foot width of a flight of steps flanked by sphinxes on pedestals (now removed) further enhanced the building which originally overlooked the parkland of the Tyndall Estate and a narrow roadway to Park Street.

Clifton could have been graced with an even more impressive Greek Revival monument in the shape of a massive new Roman Catholic church. But circumstances were heavily weighted against the ambitious project.

In 1829, the year of the Catholic Emancipation Act, Peter Augustine Baines was appointed Vicar Apostolic of the Western District. He envisaged a great basilica overlooking Bristol, one which would surpass any other contemporary Catholic place of worship in the country. Henry Edmund Goodridge (c. 1800–63), known familiarly as the architect of Lansdown Tower in Bath, had undertaken work at the College of Prior Park in Bath which had been founded by Bishop Baines and he was now appointed to design the church (see Plate 6). The foundations were laid in 1834 but work was interrupted when the ground of the steep site on Honeypen Hill shifted dangerously.

The financial burden of the project bankrupted Father Francis Edgworth, the local priest who had taken responsibility for the project. He retired to Belgium in 1845, leaving the walls and six huge portico columns at only a quarter of their intended height. The following year Bishop Ullathorne succeeded as Vicar Apostolic and determined to construct a church over Goodridge's unfinished building. Its fabric was too thin and the span too wide to support the intended tower and in view of the instability of the foundations, Ullathorne chose to construct a lightweight timber structure and roof based on shipbuilding principles. The architect asked to build to his instructions was Charles Hansom (1815/16–88). The Pro-Cathedral was to be architecturally enhanced by additions made in the 1870's by the same architect who was by then one of the leading members of the local profession (see Plate 29).

In its forceful design and archaeological attention to decoration, the Church of St. Mary-on-the-Quay (see Plate 7), can be compared with the Victoria Rooms. The architect, Richard Shackleton Pope (1781–1884), had received an appointment as District Surveyor to the Corporation in 1838. Richard was probably the son of Thomas Pope who had held the same office between 1801–5. The church, which fronted the dockside of the River Frome (now covered over), was originally designed as a chapel for the followers of the evangelist, Edward Irving. Three years after its construction in 1839–40 it was purchased by the Roman Catholics. The church's magnificent pedimented Corinthian portico raised on a lofty stylobate was an especially fine example of the temple design.

The Greek Revival may be seen as a romantic development of Neo-Classicism; so too may the early stages of the Gothic Revival.

By the early 19th century, the growth of the population and its extension into areas beyond the ancient city wards indicated an urgent need for new churches. Bristol like so many other towns in Britain was to benefit from Church Building Grants made to the Church of England through a Parliamentary Commission founded in 1818. Because of

PLATE 7

The Church of St. Mary-On-The-Quay, Colston Avenue
Richard Shackleton Pope, 1839–40.
Line engraving.   *City Art Gallery, Bristol*

Holy Trinity Church, Trinity Road, St. Philips
Thomas Rickman and
Henry Hutchinson, 1829.
Line engraving. *City Art Gallery, Bristol*

economic necessity the buildings were simple in plan. We have seen the use of the Grecian style in Smirke's Church of St. George, for which an early application was made by the authorities in the Parish of St. Augustine, but the Gothic or more particularly its later variant, the Perpendicular, was also employed.

Bristol has an outstanding example of a Gothic Commissioners' church. Holy Trinity in the parish of St. Philip and St. Jacob was designed in 1829 by Thomas Rickman (1776–1841), and his partner, Henry Hutchinson (see Plate 8). Rickman was as zealous in his archaeological approach to Gothic architecture as Smirke and Cockerell were to Greek architecture. From his Liverpool and Birmingham offices Rickman issued Gothic designs of a finer accuracy than was generally applied to the Commissioners' churches. The dominant features of Holy Trinity are the two open-traceried and embattled turrets flanking the west façade. The English style of the 15th century which Rickman characteristically chose and the simple, low pitched roof and hall-like rectilinear space were suited to the economical requirements of such churches. As with the temple plans of Greek church designs there was little differentiation between the nave and the chancel, thus allowing the congregation an easy view of the altar and pulpit. Later liturgical requirements made these early simple plans abhorrent to the Victorians.

During the 1830's and 1840's there was no single principle of design to which architects could confidently refer. Revivals of past styles were generally classified according to building types. By and large the Greek style was favoured for large public or administrative buildings, but, more and more, Gothic became the usual style for churches. Variants of Tudor or Jacobean styles were to be increasingly applied to domestic, collegiate or institutional buildings.

It was therefore possible for an architect like Charles Dyer to diversify his talents, producing, on the one hand, a design of classical opulence for the Victoria Rooms, and on the other a charming, picturesque cluster of Gothic gables, crocketed finials and oriel windows. A plan for such a building with a richly panelled interior on a site above Park Street was adopted by the trustees of the endowed school of the Red Maids in 1834. However, a new body of trustees appointed in 1836 questioned the expense and immodesty of Dyer's design. The finished building was eventually purchased by Dr. Monk, Bishop of Gloucester and Bristol who established there his Anglican school known as Bishop's College.

Adjacent to this College was the Bristol Asylum and School of Industry for the Blind, built in 1834 to designs by Thomas Rickman (see Plate 9). Here the castellated turrets and slender, lancet windows conformed to a strict Gothic style. The main wings of both institutions, together with the centrally placed Asylum chapel, were in Bath stone and must have formed a romantic E-shaped complex on the site which is now occupied by the City Museum and Art Gallery and the University buildings.

By contrast, the City School or Queen Elizabeth's Hospital, designed by Thomas Foster and Son and completd in 1847 (see Plate 10), is in the severest Tudor collegiate style. Thomas Foster had joined the partnership of James Foster and Son in 1818. This Bristol firm whose name was to change many times, was consistently productive and inventive throughout the Victorian period. The geometrical castellated blocks, formed from the hard reddish-brown stone excavated from the very site on which the school is built, are massed in a fortress-like manner making the most of the steeply rising site on the western side of Brandon Hill.

Henceforth local architects could provide the schools and institutions of the city with either modest or, where wealth permitted, exuberant domestic Gothic embellishments. Nationally established advances in fashion are acknowledged somewhat belatedly in the school buildings, parish rooms, almshouses, gatehouses and in the more substantial

Bristol Asylum and School of Industry for the Blind, Queen's Road
Thomas Rickman, 1834.
Watercolour illustration by S. C. Jones of a building demolished circa 1900.
The Wills Memorial Building of the University of Bristol now occupies this site. *City Art Gallery, Bristol*

PLATE 9

Queen Elizabeth's Hospital, Berkeley Place
Thomas Foster and Son, 1844–7.
Lithograph. *City Art Gallery, Bristol*

PLATE 10

detached houses in the new suburbs of Cotham, Redland and Clifton. The Italianate, modified Grecian, Elizabethan and Tudor houses in such roads as Clifton Park, and the gabled, bayed Jacobean residences in Cotham Road illustrate the stylistic dilemma in which local builders and architects of the late 1830's and early 1840's found themselves. The scholastic orthodoxy of the Grecian taste was gradually to be sacrificed to a desire for the freedom of hybrid styles which conveyed certain sentiments or historical associations. The stylistic confusion experienced nationally during the early Victorian period was later to be dispelled with the help of academic enquiry and of the writings of such critics as Augustus Welby Northmore Pugin (1812–52), and John Ruskin (1819–1900), by which historicism in architecture was to be endowed with new enlightened principles.

By the 1840's Bristol was graced with a small number of public buildings and churches built by both visiting and local architects in the new sophisticated Greek style. But the old city still preserved a townscape of an essentially late medieval scale and character, surrounded by fine Georgian squares and terraces. Before turning our attention to the massive building programmes of the later Victorian period, which were to transform the appearance of the commercial quarter and of the dock frontages, we must comment on buildings where the choice of style was of academic concern. Of greater significance was their specifically modern purpose. We can find in Bristol some examples of early Victorian architecture which are of national importance.

The scale of the Clifton Suspension Bridge impresses us now as one of the great modern achievements in engineering. When completed in 1864 the bridge could be regarded by Bristolians as a proud symbol of their city's awakening to a 19th century spirit of daring enterprise. In 1753 a merchant, William Vick, had bequeathed £1,100 to the Society of Merchant Venturers with the intention that it should accumulate to provide a sufficient sum for the construction of a road bridge over the Avon at Clifton.

No other project in Bristol's history has invited such an extraordinary variety of alternative designs as the competition for the Clifton Bridge. The designs were as various and often as foolish in their architectural styles as in their engineering techniques. Few Bristol architects or engineers took part. The Avon Gorge was wider at the recommended point than any space previously bridged with a single span and it was inevitably the engineers who emerged in the final round. But the winner proved himself to be a brilliant architect as well as an engineer of genius, Isambard Kingdom Brunel (1806–59).

On March 27th, 1831, Brunel wrote: " . . . I have to say that of all the wonderful feats I have performed since I have been in this part of the world I think yesterday I performed the most wonderful. I produced unanimity amongst fifteen men who were all quarrelling about the most ticklish subject—taste. . . .

"The Egyptian thing I brought down was quite extravagantly admired by *all—unanimously* adopted and I am directed to make drawings. Lithographs, etc., etc. . . ."

Only a few days earlier the Bridge Committee had pronounced Brunel the winner of the second competition and it had chiefly admired his various Gothic or castellated designs of which one was based on the gateway to Christ Church, Oxford, and another on Lancaster Castle. Four years later when the project was foundering Brunel completed detailed designs for the gateways in a Moorish style, complete with tiled roofs.

Brunel had always foreseen the dramatic possibilities of a bridge across the Avon Gorge, but the winning Egyptian design was by no means his most ambitious and romantic conception (see Plate 11). Another design was three hundred feet longer and involved approach tunnels with the bridge springing directly from the cliff face through castellated gateways set into the rock. But now the elegant gateways beautifully matched the curves and lightness of

The Clifton Suspension Bridge

PLATE 11

Brunel's victorious Egyptian design drawn in April 1831 by Brunel himself and the Bristol artist Samuel Jackson for public exhibition. The Bridge was completed in an altered and simpler form in 1864.   Watercolour.   *City Art Gallery, Bristol*

Temple Meads Station
Isambard Kingdom Brunel, 1839–41.
This building contained the booking hall,
offices and a Board Room of
the Great Western Railway Company,
whose Paddington to Bristol line
opened in June, 1841.
Lithograph.   *City Art Gallery, Bristol*

PLATE 12

PLATE 13

**The Train Shed of Temple Meads
Station**
Isambard Kingdom Brunel, 1839–41
Since 1965 trains have not used this
station. It now serves as a car park. For
an illustration of the Joint Station serving
the Midland, Bristol and Exeter and
Great Western Railway Companies,
built around 1870, and used as the station
today, see Plate 43.
Lithograph by J. C. Bourne
          City Museum, Bristol

13

the suspended bridge itself, and their shape and solidity perfectly reflected their vital strength and function. They were to be cased with cast iron reliefs illustrating the entire history of the construction of the bridge; an idea that illustrates the faith and heroic enthusiasm that accompanied the early stages of Victorian engineering. The sphinxes above the gateways face inwards. Brunel must have realised that they thus presented an unsuitable aspect for the traveller approaching the bridge and, as in most subsequent prints and paintings based upon Brunel's plans, the sphinxes are reversed.

The bridge was the foundation of Brunel's career, his earliest significant commission, "my first child", as he called it. Work began in 1831 but proceeded very slowly until, by the mid 1840's, the capital was exhausted and the half-finished abutments and towers long remained a reproach. Ironically it was Brunel's death in 1859 that inspired his colleagues in the Institute of Civil Engineers to encourage its completion as a memorial to their friend. The bridge opened on December 8th, 1864, to a much more severe design.

But the early realisation of Brunel's architectural and engineering skill could be proclaimed in the terminus built by him for the Great Western Railway Company to which he had been appointed as Chief Engineer in 1833. When the railway line between London and Bristol was opened in 1841, the terminal building was nearing its completion (see Plates 12 and 13).

The ambitious design for the station at Temple Meads was without precedent and remarkable in its stylistic unity. Brunel had followed the revival convention of civic and domestic architects in his choice of a castellated Tudor facade to the large company offices which fronted Temple Gate. Passengers passed through the flanking arches to a booking hall on the ground floor and then went upstairs to the platforms and railway which was supported on a high viaduct similar to the one at the smaller station at

Bath, designed by Brunel in 1840–41.

The facades, turrets and historically evocative decoration exemplified a type of railway architecture which contemporary critics such as Pugin and Ruskin were to consider wholly anachronistic and inappropriate. However the ingenious adaptation of the Perpendicular idiom to the "nave" and aisles of the train shed, with its enormous timber hammerbeam roof supported on arcades of Tudor arched iron columns, must certainly command our admiration today. In few important stations of a later date can one find the architectural treatment of the booking offices carried so naturally and coherently through to the body of the station.

The Royal Western Hotel in St. George's Road, now familiarly known as Brunel House, was designed in 1837 by Richard Shackleton Pope in collaboration with Brunel (see Plate 14).

Its proud Ionic colonnade, attached Corinthian columns and pavilions, reflected the courage and ambitions of both the Great Western Railway Company and the Great Western Steamship Company. This modern hotel was to accommodate passengers travelling between Bristol and America in Brunel's steamship, *The Great Western*, which had made its first transatlantic crossing in 1838. Although the Royal Western Hotel was placed at some distance from Temple Meads it served two triumphs of modern technology and stood as a symbol of a new commercial enterprise by which Bristol would form the hub of a communications system between London, the West, the Midlands and even North America. Such sentiments were expressed by the Mayor, J. K. Haberfield, when he held the chair at the public dinner marking the opening of the impressive new hotel in May 1839. He declared that Bristol was waking from its trance and he foresaw the light of better days approaching at railway speed.

Such optimism was generally proclaimed, but the decades

The Royal Western Hotel, St. George's Road

PLATE 14

Richard Shackleton Pope, 1837.
This hotel was originally planned in collaboration with Brunel as one which would serve passengers transferring from the Great Western Railway to the steamship, *The Great Western*. Through one of the arches was a "Bazaar Ride" which afforded covered accommodation for coaches. The building is now an office block known as Brunel House.   Lithograph.   *City Art Gallery, Bristol*

PLATE 15

The Guildhall, Broad Street
Richard Shackleton Pope, 1837.   Lithograph.

City Art Gallery, Bristol

which mark the beginning of Victoria's reign were economically precarious for Bristol. By the 1820's the Port had recovered from the restrictions of the Napoleonic Wars and major improvements, in the form of an entirely new tidal channel for the Avon, which was engineered in 1804-9 leaving the old course of the river as a Floating Harbour, had improved docking facilities. However, the docking fees remained inordinately high to the benefit of rival ports such as Cardiff and, or course, Liverpool, which could more efficiently meet the ever increasing requirements of modern shipping. To the satisfaction of the mercantile community and the Free Port Association, the City took control of the docks in 1848, but the narrow, severely tidal Avon Gorge was eventually to present unsurmountable difficulties to large ocean-going vessels.

Nevertheless, Bristol continued to be a major port and a city of great wealth. A number of new commercial ventures were instigated. For instance, in 1836 the Great Western Cotton Works and an enormous Sugar Refinery were built and the Bristol Steam Navigation Company was established.

In 1830 the architectural critic, John Britton, could notice in the preface of his *History and Antiquities of Bristol Cathedral*, a flourishing in the intellectual life in the city. Even though the younger untrammelled town of Liverpool might eventually surpass its veteran rival in the commercial field, in its history and antiquities Bristol was pre-eminent.

In 1843, twenty years after the building of the Greek Revival Council House, a new sense of historical pride in Bristol's past could be expressed in a very modern Victorian public building in the Gothic style.

The classically adorned masses of the Royal Western Hotel had demonstrated Pope's mastery of an up-to-the-minute architectural style which could provide a convenient, dignified edifice serving modern needs. But, in 1843, Pope, as Surveyor to the Corporation, was required to design a new Guildhall (see Plate 15) on the site of the medieval hall in Broad Street. He chose to dress the building, which accommodated various Courts of Law and rooms for the Judge, Mayor and Counsellors, in Perpendicular ornament. The choice was an exceptional one for this date. The niches between the deeply recessed and traceried windows on the first storey contained statues of Edward III, who had granted the Corporation Charter in 1373, Queen Victoria, John Dunning and Sir Michael Foster (former Recorders of the City) and Bristol's two merchant philanthropists, Colston and Whitson. Shields in the coupled quartrefoils over the windows bear the arms of eminent men connected with Bristol's history such as Cabot, Penn, Camden and Southey.

A newspaper critic commented on the turreted tower raised behind the horizontal line of the pierced parapet and projecting bay, thus anticipating the popular objection to such a feature which broke with the Classical decorum expected of public buildings of this type. He added, however, that the architect could be reassured by the precedent of the long, unbroken line of the new and similarly styled Houses of Parliament, designed by Sir Charles Barry and begun in 1839. Pope had consciously created an architectural monument to Bristol's venerable past. A "domestic" Perpendicular style was more suitable than the Greek, in the same way that the Parliament buildings had recognised Gothic as a national style. The facade moreover conformed visually to the narrowness of the ancient street in which it was placed. The statuary and emblematic detail, instead of being uncomfortably placed above the cornice line, as in such buildings as the nearby Council House, were now united with the structure of the main elevation.

CHURCH BUILDING
AND THE GOTHIC REVIVAL

The religious life of Victorian Bristol was vigorous. Private endowments to churches in prosperous areas were matched by the fervent activities of the evangelical, auxiliary and itinerant societies which were founded to keep pace with the needs of the rapidly expanding population in Bristol's surrounding villages (see Plate 18).

Architects who had worked for the Parliamentary Commissioners had chosen either Greek or Gothic styles for their church designs. But by the 1840's Gothic was to be the predominant style.

Thomas Rickman's *Attempt to Discriminate the Styles of Architecture from the Conquest to the Reformation* of 1817 had provided one of the first systematic treatises on Gothic architecture. Such publications, which appeared in the early decades of the 19th century, made it possible for ordinary people as well as dilettante scholars to appreciate the principles of the Gothic style.

In Bristol Rickman's churches, together with such others as Charles Dyer's St. Paul's, Bedminster, 1829–30, and John Hicks' St. John the Evangelist, Clifton, 1841, belong to the initial phase of the Gothic Revival, when Gothic decoration was inclined to be superimposed on to essentially Georgian structures.

By the mid 1840's there was a new purpose behind the use of Gothic; it was no longer simply a style but a principle of faith. The Gothic Revival was academically formulated and popularised by a group of Cambridge High Churchmen who had formed the Camden Society in 1839.

The Society wished to promote the study of ecclesiastical architecture and the restoration of medieval monuments. Its outspokenness on church symbolism and disapproval of old-fashioned galleries, boxed-in pews and short chancels

were voiced in its journal, *The Ecclesiologist*. The Society was to have a far-reaching influence on Anglican church building and shared with the brilliant architect and designer, Augustus Welby Northmore Pugin, a romantic passion for the glories of Gothic as the only true Christian architecture. Pugin had demonstrated in one of his more influential publications, *The True Principles of Pointed or Christian Architecture*, 1841, the inadequacy of superficial Gothic ornament unless it was a coherent part of a well understood Gothic structure.

Although Pugin was converted to the Roman Catholic faith, his convictions had an increasing appeal amongst the members of the Camden Society which was allied to the Church of England. The Tractarian movement was still more concerned with the revival of Catholic clerical offices, vestments and ritual.

Antiquarians, historians, ministers of religion and architects were henceforth to be influenced by what can broadly be described as the Ecclesiological Movement. Its first centres of activity were the university towns of Cambridge and Oxford and a suggestion of the Oxford Society for Promoting the Study of Gothic Architecture led to a local branch being formed in Bristol for the similar purpose of cultivating a correct taste for Gothic and of recording and restoring medieval antiquities in the district.

The Bristol and West of England Architectural Society was founded in 1841. It rapidly amassed archaeological literature on local monuments and, within eight years of its foundation, the Gloucester and Bristol Diocesan Church Building Society was to submit for examination all plans for new churches. The Society incorporated a small body of local architects. Men, such as John Bindon, Thomas Foster, John Hicks, Charles Dyer and Richard Shackleton

PLATE 16

The Church of St. Mark, Easton
Designed by Charles Dyer and carried out
by Samuel Burleigh Gabriel, 1848. Lithograph.   *City Art Gallery, Bristol*

The Church of St. John, Bedminster
John Norton, 1855.
Gutted during the Second World War, demolished 1965.
Lithograph.   *City Art Gallery, Bristol*

PLATE 17   19

Pope, could, for a short time, share some common purpose and inspiration.

Once again many of the new churches in Bristol were to be designed by visiting architects. But of the churches by local architects which conformed to the new ecclesiological requirements one can cite St. Jude's in Braggs Lane, St. Philip's, 1849, and St. Michael's on Two Mile Hill, Kingswood, 1848, both by Samuel Burleigh Gabriel. The same architect completed in 1848 the unusually beautiful church of St. Mark, Easton (see Plate 16), which had been designed in a Norman style by Charles Dyer, the author of the Victoria Rooms. Dyer's academic handling of different historical styles made it possible for him to produce an equally competent version of the Early English style in Clifton's Christ Church, consecrated in 1841.

Of visiting architects the most active was John Norton (1823–1904), whose churches best demonstrate contemporary ecclesiological demands. Norton was active in both the ecclesiastical and secular fields throughout the South and West of England and in South Wales. Locally, he designed such buildings as the Diocesan Training College of St. Matthias at Fishponds, in 1853, and the exotic Gothic mansion, Tyntesfield at Wraxall, erected in 1863–66 for William Gibbs.

He had trained in the Bloomsbury office of the architect, Benjamin Ferrey (1810–80), whose Early English and more favoured Decorated Gothic styles were those which Norton was to follow. The spacious ground plans, asymetrically placed towers, slender arcades, clearly defined chancels, steeply pitched timber framed roofs and a wealth of sculptural detail in the form of angels and stiff-leaf capitals are features which can be enjoyed in such surviving churches as Holy Trinity, Stapleton, 1857, and St. Mary Magdalene of 1860–64, in the park-like suburb of Stoke Bishop. Unhappily, of the two of his most impressive churches, St. Matthias-on-the-Weir, 1851, has been demolished and St. John's, Bedminster, 1855, was gutted during the Second World War (see Plate 17). However, the slender Salisbury-like spire which he added to Christ

Church, Clifton, in 1859, remains a prominent landmark.

The liturgical issues which were of such vital importance to the Camden Society were to have little effect on Non-Conformist church building. Although a strict adherence to simple rectangular plans was to be maintained, some denominations did countenance Gothic Romanesque and later Italianate embellishments in their designs.

This is demonstrated by the Bristol architect, Richard Shackleton Pope. For the Irvingites he had designed the cool and powerful Greek Chapel, now known as St. Mary-On-The-Quay, in 1839. But in 1847 Pope, with easy confidence, could grace the small Buckingham Baptist Chapel with sharply pointed blank arcading, a rose window and pinnacle-topped turrets, creating an excellent stylistic essay in the continental High Gothic manner. Furthermore the structural body of the chapel had completely broken with Classical principles and on its completion it excited general admiration (see Plate 19).

But a more significant departure from the classical tradition of Non-Conformist church design, and one of an exceptionally early date, was to be found at Highbury Chapel built on Cotham Hill. The architect was William Butterfield (1814–1900), the young nephew of the Congregationalist William Day Wills, one of the Chapel's founders. Butterfield, who had undertaken his architectural training at Worcester, where he had measured and sketched the Cathedral and local churches, had set up practice in his Adelphi office, London, in 1847, the year in which work started at Highbury (see Plate 20).

Unlike contemporary Bristol churches with their ashlar facings and crisp detail, Butterfield exploited the more random effect of local rubble stone dressed with Bath stone quoins. In 1863 the Chapel was to receive an apse, transept and tower to the designs of the young Bristol architect, Edward William Godwin (1833–88). But the Perpendicular style of Butterfield's building, with its slender piers and steeply raftered oak roof, amounted to an acknowledgment of Pugin's principles which had advocated the use of natural

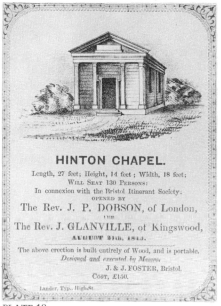

Trade card of J. & J. Foster, carpenters, St. Paul's, 1845
City Art Gallery, Bristol

PLATE 18

PLATE 19

Buckingham Baptist Chapel, Queen's Road, Clifton
Richard Shacketon Pope, 1847.
Line engraving.
City Art Gallery, Bristol

PLATE 20

Highbury Congregational Chapel, Cotham Road
William Butterfield, 1847.
In 1863 a tower, transept and apse were added by Edward William Godwin.
Lithograph. *City Art Gallery, Bristol*

PLATE 21

Reredos in the Church of St. Mary Redcliffe
Designed by George Godwin, carved in Caen stone by W. Rice, circa 1870.   Removed 1956.

The Builder, June 3rd, 1871

PLATE 22

The Cathedral of St. Augustine
The original perspective design for the proposed additions of a nave and western towers by George Edmund Street.
This design presumably accompanied ground plans and a report of 1867 which were presented to the Restoration Committee.
John Loughborough Pearson completed the towers after Street's death in 1881, but omitted the steeples.
Watercolour, pen and ink.

City Art Gallery, Bristol

materials, honest clear construction, and visible buttressing. The same characteristics were to appear within the next three years in Butterfield's nearby church and vicarage of St. Mary's, Coalpit Heath. The vicarage, with its irregular massing and unadorned stone walls, is a very important early work by this most influential Victorian architect.

In 1842 Butterfield was to establish a successful relationship with the Cambridge ecclesiologists and he then developed an original, aggressive and personal style based on the use of different coloured bricks for both construction and patterned decoration. His better known works include All Saints', Margaret Street in London and Keble College, Oxford.

One of Butterfield's few pupils, Henry Woodyer (1816–96), could show something of his master's flair for poly-chromatic decoration in such churches as Holy Innocents' at Higham in Gloucestershire, 1847. But in Bristol (see Plate 26), he was to employ the more traditional Decorated style in the Chapel of St. Raphael on the Cumberland Road by the new course of the Avon. The founder, the Reverend Robert H. Miles intended that it should serve seamen visiting the port of Bristol. It opened in 1859 and was to be the scene of much elaborate decoration and ritualist ceremonial which aroused much controversy. Attached to the chapel was an ornamental row of alms-houses for sailors' widows which, with its generously pitched tiled roofs, barge-boarded dormer windows and wooden-traceried cloister, showed how Woodyer could draw lessons from vernacular English architecture for use in a Victorian Gothic building.

In the mid-Victorian period the Gothic Revival found expression, not only in the great numbers of new churches, but in a pious attention to the restoration of medieval Gothic monuments.

In a series of lectures on architecture delivered at the Bristol Philosophical Institute in 1833, John Britton (1771–1853), the medieval archaeologist, had recommended various building improvements in the city, which included the restoration of the ancient church of St. Mary Redcliffe. Britton had already published a description of the Church in 1813 in a volume of Browne Willis' *Survey of English Cathedrals*. A succession of popular guides all celebrated the beauties of Bristol's most cherished medieval monument. But the appealing and romantic decay of "this elegant and tasteful pile" was causing concern to the church wardens who published urgent appeals for the restoration fund. The advice of John Britton was sought and the outside archi-tect, George Godwin (1815–88), who was to become the first editor of the architectural journal, *The Builder*, was appointed as surveyor in 1842. Work progressed slowly until an anonymous benefactor, Alderman Thomas Proctor, calling himself "Nil Desperandum", began to forward money for the restoration of the north porch. The financial support of the Canynge Society, founded in 1848, and of the Commercial Society, eventually made the extensive and costly restoration possible.

The opening up of the ambulatory leading to the Lady Chapel, the installation of stained-glass windows, a pulpit and a font, the repair of the stone carved decoration and the introduction of a new and highly ornate reredos (see Plate 21), allowed for the most lavish embellishment which transformed the Georgianised Gothic interior into a vigorously Victorian place of worship. Almost as much was removed as was added.

The outstanding Baroque organ casing was a notable loss, but fortunately Hogarth's vast altarpiece survives today in St. Nicholas Church Museum. The restoration culminated in the completion of the spire in 1878.

The most important ecclesiastical work to take place in Bristol during the 19th century was the building of the Cathedral Nave. The monuments of the ancient Augus-tinian Abbey had long been admired by visiting anti-quarians. But the possibility of building on the foundations of a nave, begun by Abbot Newland in the early 16th century, and thus extending the beautiful early 14th century work of Abbot Knowle, had not been seriously considered, even though an architect's impressions of a fanciful

PLATE 23

The Church of All Saints, Pembroke Road, Clifton   *City Art Gallery, Bristol*
George Edmund Street, 1864–8.
This church was gutted during the Second World War and subsequently demolished.
Watercolour by M. K. Moore, 1896.

The Church of the Holy Nativity, Knowle
Archibald Ponton and William Venn Gough, 1871–83.
The Church was destroyed in 1940 during the Blitz, and rebuilt to a
simpler design between 1954–8.   *Published design.   Circa 1880*

PLATE 24

Christ Church, Julian Road, Sneyd Park
Stuart Colman, 1877.
Demolished 1961–2.
The Building News, January 12th, 1877

PLATE 25

Perpendicular nave had been published in the 1840's.

The first stage of restoration, as opposed to reconstruction, was instigated at a meeting in the Guildhall in March 1861. The Archdeacon, Canon Norris, who had canvassed for restoration subscriptions, heightened his campaign in 1866 when excavations for the lowering of the road on the north side of the Cathedral revealed the foundations of a Norman nave. Increased donations then made it possible to invite the eminent London architect, George Edmund Street (1824–81), to supply ground plans and an elevation for the more ambitious project of constructing a nave (see Plate 22).

At a public meeting in June 1867 Street presented a report to the Restoration Committee in which he explained his plan to provide a modified continuation of Abbot Knowle's Choir, whereby the aisles would be as high as the nave and would contain tall transomed windows with strict geometrical tracery. His more personal contribution would be the introduction of Purbeck marble shafts to the piers of the nave.

The west front was to conform to an earlier phase of Gothic reminiscent of continental cathedral facades of the 13th century. Street believed that steeples would not have been envisaged by the medieval architects but he thought that their addition to the two western towers would rightly make the Cathedral a more conspicuous and impressive building. Unfortunately J. L. Pearson omitted the steeples when he completed the towers after Street's death. With great tact and scholarship Street had succeeded in designing the vast nave and western facade in sympathy with the medieval choir and tower. But in the small church of All Saints', Pembroke Road, Clifton, he allowed himself a more creative flexibility whereby he could introduce new motifs in line with advanced interpretations of the Gothic style (see Plate 23).

Street was appointed to design All Saints' Church in 1863. The church's founders had the support of the local Society for Promoting Freedom of Public Worship, which had abhorred the old pew system that had given the rich and non-resident worshippers of Clifton the monopoly of reserved seats. The Building Committee also wanted frequent services of an impressive kind and Street's designs pleased them greatly.

Before its virtual destruction during the Second World War All Saints' Church contained many beautiful features. The deeply recessed arches of the nave proudly displayed alternate bands of pink, blue and yellow stone. Rising above this massive structure was a tall clerestory containing neat rows of traceried windows all emblazoned with richly coloured stained-glass.

The loss of this church is a sad one as it could have compared with some of the most exciting experiments of other High Victorian architects. In church design Street and Butterfield, as we have already noticed, introduced novel elements of construction and decoration which overlooked the more traditional styles of English Gothic and took inspiration from continental examples.

These new departures had been partly inspired by the writings of the critic, John Ruskin, who had in his book, *The Seven Lamps of Architecture*, 1848, lifted architectural study above stylistic and liturgical issues. The inspired theoretical content of this book was to be further expounded in his second publication, *The Stones of Venice*, of 1851–3, which excited a new admiration for early Italian and especially Venetian Gothic.

In 1853 Street himself visited Italy and, following the example of Ruskin, collected notes and made sketches which enabled him, two years later, to produce his book, *The Brick and Marble Architecture of the Middle Ages*. This in its turn was to have a wide influence on both ecclesiastic and secular architecture.

By the 1860's the suburban district of Knowle had expanded to such an extent that the Vicar of St. John's, Bedminster, and Father Turton of the mission of St. Raphael's, decided to instigate plans for a new church on the Wells Road. The Church of Holy Nativity, now the

Foster's Almshouses, Colston Street
John Foster and J Wood.
Original design showing the elevation of the east wing and a
section of the southern wing of the quadrangle; dated 1872. These
additions were made to an earlier western wing begun after 1861.
Also shown are proposed embellishments for the facade of the 16th
century Chapel of the Three Kings of Cologne, carried out in a
simpler form. *Bristol Record Office*

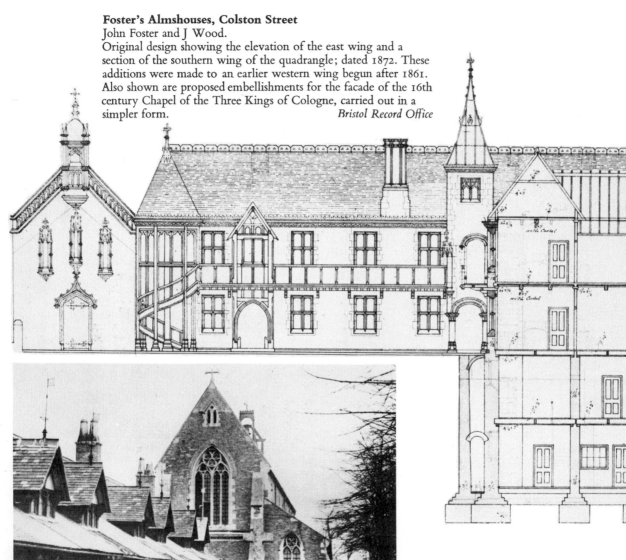

PLATE 27

St. Raphael's Chapel and Almshouses, Cumberland Road
Henry Woodyer, 1859.
The chapel was destroyed during the Second World War.
The almshouses have been demolished in recent years.
Avon County Library, Bristol

28

PLATE 26

parish church of Knowle, was designed by the local architect, William Venn Gough, in partnership with Archibald Ponton, and was consecrated in 1883 (see Plate 24). The prominent red brick tower was not completed until 1931 and the banded polychromatic lower portion is all that remains to suggest the original character of the building.

The firm of Ponton and Gough produced much of the city's interesting commercial architecture in the same robust spirit. The use of red and yellow Bridgwater bricks, strong horizontal and geometrical patternings and even the intention of covering the chancel apse with mosaic, indicate the confident and modern adaptation of an early Christian basilican plan, illustrations of which were available to these architects through the medium of professional journals and other more academic publications.

By the 1870's the spirited discipline of the Gothic Revival had lost its force. Faced with a profusion of styles, architects could diversify their talents and indulge in personal tastes. Stuart Colman was a newcomer to the Bristol architectural scene. In his David Thomas Memorial Church built at Bishopston for the Congregationalists in 1881 and in his unfortunately now demolished Christ Church at Sneyd Park of 1877 (see Plate 25) could be seen his predeliction for slender, attenuated turrets and spires and a freakish arrangement of triple lancet windows.

Bristol's ecclesiastical architecture of the mid-Victorian period clearly owes more to outside architects. But the impact of the Gothic Revival in the secular field is best seen in several outstanding buildings by members of the local profession.

The Bristol and West of England Architectural Society, which had for a decade or so united a small group of local architects, could, by the 1850's, no longer function co-operatively in propagating the true style of Gothic. It was, in fact, superseded by the Bristol Society of Architects, founded in 1850 as the second of the Allied Societies of the Royal Institute of British Architects. The new Society turned its attention to professional matters and the establishment of a code of practice. It held to no particular philosophy and its members were permitted a freedom of aesthetic choice.

Charles Underwood and Richard Shackleton Pope and his partners, Bindon and Clark, favoured classically based styles. John Foster, who we can presume to be the son of Thomas Foster, and John's partner, Joseph Wood, employed an imaginative Gothic spirit in their designs for schools and almshouses, which, in their enthusiastic attention to decorative detail, far surpassed the comparable but tame and sparingly Gothic parochial schools and institutions designed by their contemporaries. Trinity Almshouses, on Old Market Street, were built in three phases between 1857 and 1881 and Fosters' Almshouses, on Colston Street (see Plate 27), were built in two phases between 1861 and 1883. Both groups are Tudor in design but in their gabled porches, crocketed finials, external spiral staircases, traceried galleries and diaper patterned brickwork, they reveal a delight in the study of the most picturesque French and specifically Burgundian domestic Gothic. Foster and Wood could also instill great charm into a Gothic chapel built for the Wesleyan Methodists in 1863. Victoria Chapel at the very beginning of the Whiteladies Road must be one of our prettiest 19th century churches.

John Foster was to use the decorative forms of many different periods and countries with great sensitivity and understanding. His use of Gothic in the secular field was particularly apt as we can see in a building which was erected in Queens Road to serve the joint bodies of the Bristol Library and Philosophical Institution. After its completion in 1871, it was called the Bristol Museum and Library.

The design and plans were drawn up by John Foster and Archibald Ponton in 1866 (see the cover illustration). Foster himself designed the exterior. No greater homage could be paid to Ruskin and his celebration of Venetian Gothic. When a similar project for a Science Museum was undertaken in Oxford in 1852, a design in Veronese Gothic by Benjamin Woodward had been supported by Ruskin

PLATE 28

Clifton College

Charles Francis Hansom, 1860–6.

The tower in the centre of the quadrangle was not built as shown but altered to form a projecting bay. The Chapel to the right was to receive a north aisle in 1881 and a lantern tower in 1909.   Line engraving.

City Art Gallery, Bristol

Roman Catholic Pro-Cathedral, Park Place, Clifton
Charles Francis Hansom, 1870–6.
Published design of additions to the temporary structure built by
Hansom in 1848. The tower was never built.

PLATE 29

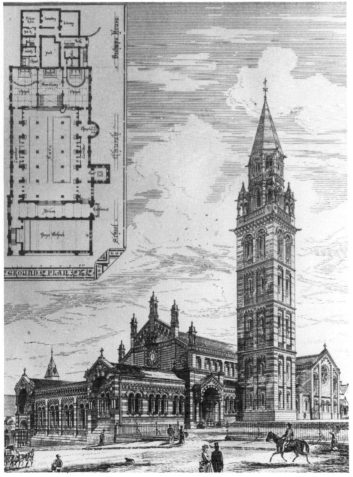

PLATE 30

**Drinking Fountain, at the Junction of Bridge Valley Road
and Clifton Down**
George and Henry Godwin, 1872.   *The Builder, August 3rd, 1872*

himself when he proclaimed the suitability of Gothic for such secular buildings.

Many of the rich decorative embellishments in imitation of those on the Doge's Palace in Venice were destroyed during the Blitz, but the lively and naturalistic carving of foliage, animals and birds covering the capitals, survives. The variety and quality of the decorative work reflects the attempt to revive not only the appearance but the ideals and techniques of medieval craftsmanship. The local Farley Down stone and red stone of Bradford-on-Avon, and the fanciful decoration around the traceried windows and seven-arched colonnade combined to delight the eye. It was appropriate that a splendid new palace of erudition and culture should be formed from such an historically evocative style. Moreover, the "modern" style of Gothic as opposed to the classicism of the British Museum, for example, reflected a new attitude towards an investigation of the natural sciences. The museum would not only be a repository of antique remains.

John Foster was to share his preference for Gothic with a fellow member of the Bristol Society of Architects, Charles Francis Hansom (1815/16–89), whose initial association with the Pro-Cathedral in Clifton has already been described. In the 1870's ambitious plans for the Pro-Cathedral's completion were revived (see Plate 29). A new facade, schoolroom and entrance portico in a North Italian Romanesque style soon distinguished the Roman Catholic building from the ecclesiological Gothic of surrounding Anglican churches. The plan for a two-hundred foot high campanile above a baptistery was never realised.

Unlike John Foster, Hansom was morally committed to the Gothic style. He had received a professional training in the office of his elder brother, Joseph Aloysius Hansom (1803–82). While in this large Roman Catholic practice in the Midlands, he had designed churches at Woodchester, Cheltenham and Wolverhampton. In 1860 Hansom was chosen to design a new public school for the Clifton College Company. It was felt that only an architect with the experience of designing in the purest Gothic could create an environment perfectly suited to the rigorous education of Christian gentlemen (see Plate 28).

The complex of buildings was developed slowly. Big School and the Headmaster's House were opened in 1862. The Chapel with its detached spire was designed in an earlier Gothic style than the secular buildings and was completed by 1866. Sympathetic additions to the College complex were made throughout the 19th century and up to the 1920's. A comparison can be made between Clifton and Malvern Colleges, where Hansom adapted a similar plan to a steeply shelving site in 1862. Much of Hansom's work at Clifton has an impressive simplicity. It was in the careful relationship of the various buildings that variety and vitality were achieved.

Instances of Gothic in the rapidly expanding residential neighbourhood of Clifton were few. A small number of tall gabled houses, in sympathy with the College were erected nearby in the 1860's and 1870's, probably to designs by Hansom. In 1860 Charles' brother, Joseph Hansom, had designed his own red brick Gothic house in Wetherall Place, Clifton, although he may never have occupied it. Two houses opposite Worcester Terrace are fine Gothic buildings, once used by the College as a sanatorium, but from the 1860's the block-like Italianate detached and semi-detached houses of the speculative builders were encroaching on all sides of the College Close.

One of Bristol's most fanciful Gothic monuments is the shrine-like drinking fountain erected on the site of the old Clifton Turnpike at the edge of the Downs (see Plate 30). It was a gift to the people of Bristol from Alderman Thomas Proctor, who, as "Nil Desperandum", had initiated the restoration of the Church of St. Mary Redcliffe. The same London architect, George Godwin, together with his brother Henry, was employed in 1872. Proctor intended the fountain to commemorate the gift of certain rights over Clifton Down made to the citizens by the Society of Merchant Venturers. Today it is a rare survival in Bristol of the mid-Victorian movement for the erection of drinking fountains.

HIGH VICTORIAN COMMERCIAL
AND PUBLIC BUILDINGS

We have already noted the formation in 1850 of the Bristol Society of Architects. This small professional body now existed to meet the growing demands of commercial expansion and we shall find an increasing number of major projects being undertaken by local architects. The membership of the Society was primarily drawn from the eighteen or so firms in Bristol and it was comprised of Fellows, Graduates and Students and a class of Associates with which engineers, surveyors, and builders were identified. This latter section gradually decreased in number, as the architects became increasingly absorbed in the establishment of their professional prerogatives. But under an alliance with the Bristol Academy of Fine Arts and under the dual presidency of John Scandrett Harford, the Society was firmly established. Its first joint activity was the building, in 1854, of new premises for the Academy on Queen's Road, in which the Society would be furnished with a meeting room (see Plate 32). The choice of style was an interesting one. The more conservative academicians favoured the Greek Revival while the architects preferred a more flexible Italian style. After a friendly competition among the members, John Hirst's Italian facade was adopted. Charles Underwood, provided the Greek fittings for the interior galleries.

The choice of the Italian style was a wise and fashionable one. No Greek building could have effectively competed with the nearby Victoria Rooms. But the colonnaded facade approached by wide flights of balustraded steps (removed in 1912) was impressive and the arched sculpture-filled recesses and the niches containing figures of Reynolds and Flaxman, appropriate for such an academic building, could not have been so easily incorporated into a temple facade.

We must remember that the later Ruskinian ideals of the Gothic Revival, illustrated sixteen years later in a similar cultural institution, the Bristol Museum and Library, had not then taken hold.

From the 1850's the revived High Renaissance taste was making headway. Scholarly classical palaces in the form of libraries, factories and warehouses were being introduced into the prosperous Northern cities. In London the taste was exemplified by the clubs in Pall Mall of which Charles Barry's Palladian Reform Club of 1838–40 was one of the earliest. In Bristol a fine example of this type of building appeared in 1857 in the West of England and South Wales Bank, in Corn Street (see Plate 31). Three years earlier the famous coaching inn, the Bush Hotel, had been purchased for £10,000. It was demolished and a magnificent new bank was erected to designs by the local architect, William Bruce Gingell (1819–1900), and T. R. Lysaght.

Like Sydney Smirke's Carlton Club House, Pall Mall, of 1847, the designs were based on the Library of St. Mark's, Venice, by the 16th century Renaissance architect, Jacopo Sansovino. Both buildings display an articulated wall facade with life-size figure sculpture in the spandrels. Bristol's bank is a small five-bayed version. The deep

The West of England and South Wales Bank, Corn Street
William Bruce Gingell and T. R. Lysaght, 1854–8.
Now Lloyds Bank Limited. The sculptural decoration was by John Evan Thomas. A later additional bay to the east incorporates a new entrance.
Engraving. *City Art Gallery, Bristol*

PLATE 31

The Bristol Academy of Fine Arts, Queen's Road
John Henry Hirst and Charles Underwood, 1854–7.
Now known as the Royal West of England Academy. The sculpture was by John Evan Thomas. The flights of steps were removed in the course of alterations by S. S. Reay in 1912.
Engraving. *City Art Gallery, Bristol*

PLATE 32

recession of the arcading and the combination of Bath and Portland stone throws the emblematic sculpture by John Evan Thomas (1809–73), into greater prominence. Every virtuosity is displayed. The figures represent the elements and sources of wealth and the frieze contains groups of boys receiving, paying, storing and coining money and printing notes. Merchants trade with exotic natives of the four Continents and the city arms of the Bank's various branches are included. Lavish sculptural decoration of this kind could be compared with the works John Thomas had submitted to the Great Exhibition held in 1851. That exhibition, in itself, had demonstrated a desire for opulent decoration which would rival the artistic splendours of the Second Empire in France.

Gingell was to make a vast contribution to the commercial and industrial architecture of the City during the latter half of the 19th century. If John Foster was Bristol's most attractive local architect, Gingell was certainly the most progressive.

He was articled to a Bath architect, J. Wilson, in 1844 and went into partnership with a fellow pupil, T. Fuller, in 1848. Together they designed St. George's Hall in Stonehouse, Devon, the Borough Prison in Plymouth and the British Lying-in Hospital in London. But his first major work was the new Bristol General Hospital (see Plate 34).

During the 1840's the annual reports of the hospital in Guinea Street had indicated the urgent need for an enlarged establishment to meet the needs of the fast increasing urban population. The reports mentioned the many new factories, the docks and the Bedminster and Ashton collieries, casualties from which constantly required surgical attention. It was decided to rebuild on the Guinea Street site which was then considered to be a healthy one. It was surrounded by water, rather than by congested smoke-filled industrial streets.

The architectural design of the building is interesting from many points of view. Gingell was appointed after a competition in 1852 and the style he chose could loosely be described as plain Italian with an asymmetrically placed polygonal corner tower capped by a curvilinear dome. Other features such as the massing of the wings and the introduction of the high dormered mansard roofs suggest, but do not corroborate, the influence of the Great Western Hotel at Paddington, designed by Philip Charles Hardwick a year earlier. It was then the grandest hotel in London, and built in a new style which was to be closely paralleled by the lavish new Louvre buildings, conceived in 1852 by J. T. Visconti and begun in 1854.

But the Hospital is less pretentious in its effect than the Hotel which had a smooth cement coating. The choice of random blue Pennant stone for the walls and the light coloured Bath stone dressings, was a formula which was to be successfully repeated in many types of mid-Victorian buildings in Bristol, and in the General Hospital it was to give a robust and dignified effect. Of greater importance was the rugged lower basement storey which enhanced the elevation of the facade and tower. Here roughly hewn Pennant stone was used, the length of the basement being relieved with small groups of round-headed windows and deeply recessed archways with massive voussoirs of Bath stone. Not only an architectural feature, the basement provided a warehouse storage area and street level entrances for the hospital. The building itself was functionally very advanced with a fireproof construction, hard cement floors and dados, elaborate heating and ventilating systems, speaking tubes and a steam-operated lift.

Gingell's use of the boldly rusticated arches and the groupings of small arched windows was of crucial stylistic

Former Warehouse of J. & R. Bush, Prince Street

PLATE 33

Architect unknown, circa 1835.
This warehouse was probably built in two stages. The earliest part can be seen in paintings by the local artist, Joseph Walter, dated 1836 and 1837.
This photograph of about 1880, was taken from the tower of St. Mary Redcliffe, and shows part of the Floating Harbour by The Grove. The
Cathedral, Brandon Hill and Clifton Hill are seen beyond. *City Art Gallery, Bristol*

PLATE 34

Bristol General Hospital, Guinea Street near Bathurst Basin
William Bruce Gingell, 1852–7.
Original design. A southern wing by the firm of Oatley and Lawrence was added in 1912 over the terraced extension of the warehouse
basement. The dome on the tower has been removed.   Watercolour.   *City Art Gallery, Bristol*

significance for the development of Bristol's factories and warehouses. The now demolished warehouse, Number 12, Temple Street (see Plate 35), can be attributed to Gingell and it was probably built soon after the completion of the General Hospital in 1857.

At this time the architects of factories and warehouses were struggling with the problems of combining a functional arrangement with an architectural treatment. In Number 12 a coherent system was applied. It is certainly Italian and Romanesque in spirit and can be compared with another famous surviving monument to the Bristol style in the form of an office block in Stokes Croft, originally built in 1862 as a carriage and harness factory for John Perry and Sons (see Plate 36). This building has three storeys of continuous arcading. Both buildings use the local combination of Pennant and Bath stone and both display horizontal string courses in a way which described the interior levels. No central visual point is stressed.

The architect of the Stokes Croft building was Edward William Godwin (1833–86), the son of a Bristol decorator. He had received his training in the office of William Armstrong, a City Surveyor and engineer, whose building style was entirely traditional. Godwin developed an early interest in medieval archaeology and, in 1851, together with W. C. Burder and James Hine, he published *The Architectural Antiquities of Bristol and its Neighbourhood*. In the same year he was elected a student member of the Bristol Society of Architects. Among his first projects was a church in County Donegal and a small, now demolished warehouse in Merchant Street, Bristol, built in 1858.

This warehouse was a gabled Gothic building with an arrangement of pointed arches which showed a practical adaptation of the medieval domestic style. In 1861, the year before Godwin designed the carriage works, he had

received his first major commission. His designs for the Town Hall at Northampton reveal the same use of continuous arcading, but in a more ornate 13th century Gothic style. On the strength of this success, Godwin was to design another Gothic town hall for Congleton in 1864, the year in which he entered into a partnership with the Bristol architect, Henry Crisp.

Designs of 1861 for a parish school for St. Philip and St. Jacob, now in the Bristol Record Office, and another of 1867 for a warehouse for the Bristol tea merchant William Polglaze, now in the Drawings Collection of the Royal Institute of British Architects, reveal a similar use of shallow round-headed arches, arcading and decorative brickwork.

The national reputation, which Godwin was to acquire, was based on his involvement with the most exciting art developments of the later Victorian period and not on his earlier work in Bristol. But his temporary relationship with the Bristol Society of Architects, to which he was elected a Fellow in 1862, was an interesting one. As Secretary and Librarian he infected the members with his own passion for medieval antiquities to the point of instigating, in 1865, an alteration of the Society's title to that of the Bristol Architectural and Archaeological Society. After Godwin's final departure from Bristol in 1871, when his partnership with Crisp ended, such corporate enthusiasm for the extra-professional matters of architecture seemed to have dwindled.

During the 1860's and 1870's the architects and builders of Bristol continued to produce works in this peculiarly local style, known popularly as "Bristol Byzantine". In an article in the *Listener* (December 2nd, 1948), Sir John Summerson drew attention to the bold round-arched style of the warehouses and related it to the Romanesque and Byzantine architecture of North Italy. But as yet no

104, Stokes Croft
Edward William Godwin, 1862.
19th century photograph of the
carriage and harness factory built for
John Perry and Sons. This building
now serves as an office block and the
bays of the lower storey contain
windows.
Reece Winstone

**W. J. Rogers, Jacob Street Brewery,
St. Philips**
Attributed to William Bruce Gingell,
circa 1865.
The offices of the Brewery fronted Old
Market Street. These have been
demolished and built over. The building
which we see here has survived in a
slightly altered form and is now a
warehouse.
*Regional Buildings Record, University of
Bath*

PLATE 35

PLATE 37

12, Temple Street
Attributed to William Bruce Gingell,
circa 1860.
Demolished.   *Regional Buildings Record,
University of Bath*

PLATE 36

The Granary, Welsh Back
Archibald Ponton and William Venn Gough, 1871.

The Builder, June 3rd, 1871.

PLATE 38

Chemist's Shop, High Street
Archibald Ponton and William Venn Gough, circa 1869.
Demolished.   *The Builder, October 2nd, 1869*

PLATE 39

evidence of the opinions of the architects themselves on this relationship has been traced. The stylistic unity of these commercial buildings appears to emanate from the fine examples of Gingell's Temple Street warehouse and Godwin's building in Stokes Croft.

Two other examples of Gingell's work are the former Christopher Thomas Soap Factory in Straight Street, off Broad Plain, and the nearby Jacob Street Brewery (see Plate 37). Both display huge rock faced arches and in the latter building, as Sir Nikolaus Pevsner has pointed out, the massive treatment of Romanesque forms is similar to that of the commercial architecture of Boston on which the American architect, Henry Hobson Richardson (1838–86), formed his style. It is perhaps our present day enthusiasm for industrial archaeology and for American commercial architecture which has in recent years inspired our critical admiration of these Bristol buildings.

We have so far discussed commercial buildings of the 1850's and 1860's which incorporated Pennant stone or rubble in their heavily rusticated lower storeys and arches; definition and patterning were stressed by the use of Bath or red Mansfield stone dressings. During the mid Victorian period these local materials were combined in an easy and dignified rhythm of arcading to give maximum impact to an often confined street frontage.

By contrast the earliest 19th century warehouses such as the surviving one in Denmark Street, had employed a simpler, functional, system of lighting the many storeys of their block-like structures by means of punctuating the thick rough stone walls with small evenly spaced windows. Such buildings were to be increasingly enhanced by a simple articulation of the exterior wall surface. The small Wool Hall in St. Thomas's Street, built by Richard Shackleton Pope about 1830, possesses a high rusticated ground floor

and a small pediment, retaining here a Georgian sense of proportion. This building displays tall round-headed recesses containing small windows. Blind arcading was to occur again in two larger and similarly styled stone warehouses of the mid 1830's. The now demolished Phillips warehouse in Charlotte Street and the former J. and R. Bush tea warehouse in Prince Street (see Plate 33) must have provided impressive and conspicuous models for the more elaborate forms of round-headed arcading which were to be used so extensively in Bristol. Today the Bush warehouse survives as one of the most outstanding commercial buildings of the early 19th century—its future assured by its timely conversion, within the original fabric, by the J.T. Group into offices and an arts complex.

We have already mentioned the firm of Ponton and Gough in connection with the Church of the Holy Nativity, Knowle. Their contribution to the commercial architecture of Bristol in the form of the Granary on Welsh Back, built in 1871 for Messrs. Wait and James, represents the apotheosis of the Bristol style (see Plate 38). The patterned brickwork openings in the ten-storey building were necessary for ventilation. The unpierced corners of the building are explained by a contemporary notice in *The Builder:*

"The great difficulty generally experienced in designing the usual external lifts and external doors on each floor has been avoided by arranging the lifts in [internal] niches at the angle of the building and by delivering the sacks of grain into carts upon moveable skids, sliding out of the round holes under the first floor string course."

The choice of the locally produced and hard Cattybrook bricks and such inventive patterning prefigured the extensive use of these bricks in many commercial and industrial buildings during later years of the century.

PLATE 40

Bristol Waggon Works, Victoria Street
Henry Crisp, 1871.
Demolished.
Avon Branch of the R.I.B.A., Bristol Society of Architects

**The former offices of the firm of
E. S. & A. Robinson Limited,
Victoria Street**
William Bruce Gingell, 1876.
Original pen, ink and watercolour design. This
building was partially destroyed by fire in 1903
and rebuilt by the Bristol firm of Oatley and
Lawrence. It was demolished in 1961 to make
way for the present building.
The Dickinson Robinson Group Limited

PLATE 41

PLATE 42

Victoria Street
Late 19th century photograph showing
the junction with Temple Street and
the tower of Temple Church.
City Art Gallery, Bristol

PLATE 43

Temple Meads Station
Sir Matthew Digby Wyatt
was architectural adviser to
the Bristol and Exeter,
Midland and Great Western
Railway Companies which
co-operated in the building of
a Joint Station between 1865
and 1878. It was built on the
site of the old Bristol and
Exeter station. To the left is
the original Great Western
Railway Station by I. K.
Brunel (see Plates 12 and 13)
to the right is the office
building of the Bristol and
Exeter Railway Company by
S. C. Fripp, 1852. The roof
of the clock tower was
destroyed during the Blitz.
Late 19th century photograph.
City Art Gallery, Bristol

The smaller scale warehouses requiring a more economic form of decoration could display arrangements of different coloured bricks with great nicety and distinction. The dockside warehouses of the 1870's by the Bathurst Basin incorporated in their facades a red and yellow pattern of Venetian ogee ornament within shallow blind arcading. One of the features of this peculiarly local idiom is its reliance on rich flat decoration and the repetition of a simple motif.

The tall factories and warehouses, in which red brick is used on a massive scale, can evoke the medieval palaces of northern Italy. The Granary with its split turrets and Gothic arched ground storey, certainly achieves this effect as does the former factory of the Christopher Thomas and Brothers Soap Works on Broad Plain, built about 1881 within the previously mentioned complex of earlier factories designed by W. B. Gingell. Although the appearance of the castellated angle turrets, traditionally prompted by the owner's visit to Florence, has since been modified, the building still provides a dominating landmark for this quarter of the city.

The arcuated style was not confined to warehouse architecture. Ponton and Gough also built the surviving Bristol Chambers in St. Nicholas Street about 1866 in which there is the early introduction of continuous round-headed arcading adapted, in the most functional way, to provide light equally for similar sized offices. The building is faced in stone and ornamental dragons appear in the spandrels.

A few years later the same firm built a splendid chemist's shop in the High Street (see Plate 39) for T. C. Pointing which must have overpowered its 17th and 18th century neighbours. By the 1860's Gothic had lost its Puginesque associations and with the publication of Ruskin's *The Stones of Venice* in 1853, architects could demonstrate to their commercial clients that arcuated North Italian Gothic had been the style of the great Venetian merchants. Mr. Pointing's desire for opulent and colourful decoration was met by Ponton and Gough who also provided deeply recessed plate-glass windows. Such visually uncomfortable combinations were to be deplored by later architectural critics.

In 1870 a new commercial thoroughfare between Temple Meads Station and the City was forged through the midst of a mass of late medieval buildings. Within the space of five years a great variety of buildings was to be erected subject to a restrictive covenant which required the facades to be of brick. G. E. Street's *The Brick and Marble Architecture of the Middle Ages*, 1855, provided the ideal pattern book for these various Italianate facades (see Plate 42).

Two buildings of particular distinction were constructed along this street and both have been demolished. In 1871 Henry Crisp designed the Bristol Waggon Works which displayed a giant arcade and polychromatic brick patterning (see Plate 40), and in 1876 Gingell designed new premises for the packaging and printing business of E. S. & A. Robinson by the Bristol Bridge. The dome was similar to the one which once graced the tower of the General Hospital (see Plate 41).

In an article in *The Architect* of 4th September, 1875, E. W. Godwin, who was practising in London, felt moved to correct the erroneous descriptions of medieval Bristol which had been published on the occasion of a visit of the British Association. His personal knowledge of Bristol and his Fellowship of the Society of Antiquaries qualified him to do so. His love for the ancient city aroused in him an abhorrence of the Victoria Street development with its dull corniced skyline: "the vulgar pretensions of uncultivated minds have overrun the city and neighbourhood,

The Colston Hall, Colston Street

John Foster and Joseph Wood, opened 1867.
Original watercolour design for the interior
of the Great Hall. It was designed to provide
seating accommodation for 3,000. The
columns, capitals and dados were of Bath
stone, the decorative features above being
finished with painted plasterwork. The Hall
was destroyed by fire in 1898, rebuilt and
re-opened in 1900 and altered and enlarged
during the 20th century.
City Art Gallery, Bristol

The Facade and Staircase of the Colston Hall

John Foster and J. Wood, completed 1873.
This building which contained the entrance hall, a
double staircase, a smaller hall and refreshment room
was connected with the Great Hall but formed a second
building stage in a simpler "Byzantine" style. The
staircase no longer exists as illustrated here and the facade
has since received a glass canopy.
Engraving.　　　*Victoria and Albert Museum (E. 654–98)*

PLATE 44

PLATE 45

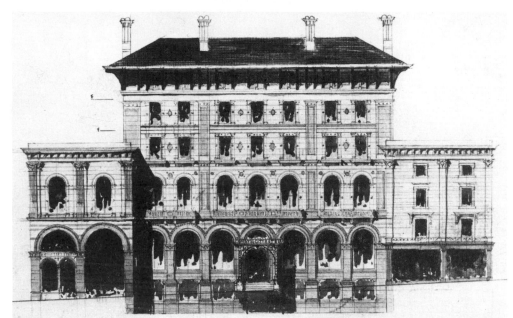

The Grand Hotel, Broad Street
John Foster and J. Wood,
opened 1869.
Original sketch design. The hotel was
built to a slightly altered design on the
site of the old White Lion and White
Hart Hotels. The pilasters were not
included and the roof-line was
subsequently altered. The lower storey
received ranges of shops to either side of
the central entrance. The building to the
left which contained an arched entrance
to Newmarket Passage has been
removed.
The Grand Hotel Company (Bristol) Limited

PLATE 46

**Offices of W. D. & H. O. Wills,
Redcliffe Street**
John Foster and J. Wood, 1869.
Demolished.
Regional Buildings Record, University of Bath

PLATE 47

PLATE 48

Assize Courts, Small Street
T. S. Pope and J. Bindon, 1867–70.
Published illustration after a design which was awarded first place in the third competition for new Assize Courts held in 1867.
The present day building conforms to this design.   *Victoria and Albert Museum (E.2307–1900)*

Gothic or Classic, it matters little which style has been selected as each has been equally abused. And if it was not for Mr. Street's work and an occasional bit from Mr. Foster, the town would be given over to a higgeldy-piggeldy of inconsistencies."

We have already noted some of Foster and Wood's outstanding work in the context of the Gothic Revival. But there were three other buildings of which Godwin might have been thinking.

In 1861 the Colston Hall Company was founded with the intention of providing the City with a large hall for meetings and concerts. In the same year the Company bought and demolished the old Carmelite Priory in St. Augustine's Place, once occupied by Colston's School. On this site the main hall (see Plate 44) was opened in 1867, with a second stage being completed in 1873. Foster and Wood had been provided with the opportunity of designing the most lavishly appointed public building in Bristol. The hall was one hundred and fifty feet long and eighty feet wide and it bore a close resemblance to the monumental St. George's Hall in Liverpool by Harvey Lonsdale Elmes (1814–47), the interior fittings of which were designed by C. R. Cockerell in 1851.

Bristol's Colston Hall was aesthetically and financially very ambitious. The hall's interior displayed a remarkably rich synthesis of Byzantine and High Renaissance styles. But the costs far exceeded the resources of the Company. The colonnaded facade, entrance hall and double staircase were consequently designed in a more restrained style (see Plate 45). The hall was destroyed by fire in 1898 but it was reconstructed and serves today as a concert hall.

In 1869 Foster and Wood again exceeded their estimates by several thousand pounds. The Grand Hotel in Broad Street received an early Renaissance facade with a large and boldly projecting cornice overshadowing an open loggia or gallery in which were placed freestone pillars and carved capitals. The impressiveness of an early design for this building (see Plate 46), was later reduced by the introduction of a range of iron and glass shops raised to the first storey of the elevation, presumably in an attempt to recover building costs.

The heavy eaves of the Grand Hotel appeared in another Foster and Wood design of 1869 for the Redcliffe Street Offices of W. D. and H. O. Wills, the tobacco manufacturers (see Plate 47). Here the elevation was formed of four storeys all of equal height, except for the uppermost one. But in place of an arcuated brick or stone arrangement, the open loggia of the Grand Hotel's top storey was employed on all levels. The deep pilasters and free-standing columns, richly decorated with lotus, bird and foliate capitals, formed an open veil-like structure behind which the "walls" of glass were hung. A development from this building would have been a very exciting one but Foster and Wood's exotic tastes and pretentions to styles of an advanced type were to be overtaken by demands for more economic brick facades in imitation of pre-formulated Italianate styles.

It must be remembered that along with the Italianate Gothic or debased Byzantine developments in the Victoria Street, Temple Street and Redcliffe Way area, builders, such as Henry Masters and James Adams Clark, could produce, throughout the City, small scale commercial premises which showed little of the Gothic Revival and no coherent adaptation of the arcuated styles. It was as though Georgian street planning had survived, but the facades were being dressed with Italianate or French embellishments.

E. W. Godwin had had no qualms in pointing out that the

PLATE 49

Corn Exchange, Corn Street
Original watercolour design for the addition by Edward Middleton Barry of an upper storey and a glass roof to the colonnaded piazza of
the Corn Exchange designed by J. Wood the Elder and built 1740–3. Barry's design was carried out and completed by 1872. In 1949 the glass
roof was removed and replaced by a shallower one which sprung from the cornice level of Wood's colonnade. *City Art Gallery, Bristol*

merchants, while they were liberal in their restoration of the more famous churches, showed no aesthetic care for the modern city which was developing around them.

Godwin's inspired approach had an historian's bias and he could see little originality in the better commercial works we have just discussed. The street architecture which he would have preferred can be visualised from his few designs and buildings which have survived. The flat decorative treatment and effective repetition of simple but craftsmanlike decoration in his warehouse designs and, especially, in the above-mentioned one for a tea merchant in Small Street, would have been far more consistent with the narrow streets of the old city than the overbearing Classical and Baroque bank and insurance company facades whose restricted sites prevented them from being set off to full advantage.

But Godwin had left his native city far behind him and Bristol was in no position to take advantage of his advanced ideals. Furthermore, Bristol's financial climate curtailed the development of any local school of architecture which could perpetuate the style and confidence of such architects as Foster and Wood. Bristol was even to engender the contempt of the national architectural press.

An unfortunate handling of competitions for new Assize Courts in Small Street in 1866 and 1867 had exasperated the local architects. The Corporation's first advertisement for designs and plans offered no guarantee of acceptance or of any premiums. The plans were to be for one of two sites either in Small Street or in the middle of Queen Square. The architects expressed their objections to this advertisement and only one set of plans was submitted.

The Council finally settled on the Small Street site, which would incorporate and preserve a 13th century hall-house.

It then instigated a competition in which the assessor, Alfred Waterhouse, recommended first, second and third premiums to three differing designs from the firm of Godwin and Crisp. E. W. Godwin's winning design was described as "vigorous and effective" and adhered strictly to the conditions of the advertisement. But the Council then reconsidered and thought it advantageous to acquire property nearby for an enlarged building to be constructed. In the face of much anger from the Presidents of the Royal Institute of British Architects and of the Bristol Society of Architects they decided to hold a third competition in which George Edmund Street was to act as adjudicator. Godwin and Crisp entered and were awarded the second premium but the firm of Popes and Bindon were the winners and the Assize Courts were constructed to the design of T. S. Pope (see Plate 48). Street admired Godwin's Gothic elevation but was impressed by the more economic plan of Popes and Bindon. It was of a less adventurous Perpendicular Gothic. The new building was to back on to the Guildhall in Broad Street built by Pope's father, Richard Shackleton Pope, twenty-five years earlier.

A happier event was the provision of a glass roof for the colonnaded courtyard of John Wood's Corn Exchange of 1741, the most magnificent 18th century building in Bristol. Wood had originally intended that the piazza should be covered to form a hall but the conservative merchants, used to trading in the open, objected. By 1869 they had changed their minds and memorialised the corporation with a request for protection from the weather. The Corporation consulted Edward Middleton Barry (1830–80), son of the more famous Charles Barry. In the early 1860's E. M. Barry had worked on the terminal stations of Charing Cross and Cannon Street. The new offices and roof of Bristol's Corn Exchange were constructed to his designs in 1872. The sculptural decoration and caryatids were executed by E. W. Wynn (see Plate 49).

HOUSING

A writer in *The Builder* (16th October, 1869), suggested that Bristol's problems of communication by water and rail had recently been solved and that the city was developing a second youth whose spirit was witnessed by so many impressive new buildings. But the most spectacular expansion could be seen in the residential areas.

The speculation was on a grand scale and it was reported in 1867 that three hundred houses in Redland, extending to the Horfield Road area, were to be erected in one scheme alone. Throughout Redland and Cotham, there was constant building of small detached villas or closely spaced semi-detached blocks in an endless variety of the Greek, Italianate or Jacobean styles. The houses were either stucco or ashlar faced, with coupled or triple round-headed windows, and shallow, stone-walled garden frontages. Road improvement schemes in Colston Street, Park Street and the cutting of Upper Maudlin Street occurred during these years and provided improved communications.

From the sub-Georgian terraces of St. Paul's into the City Road area one can still trace the elaboration from the simple Regency terraces with their neat divisional pilasters to the later Victorian type with window and door embellishments and their use of heavy bands or string courses which give a geometric pattern to long terraces. At a later date the continuous cornices were broken and bay windows and pre-moulded surface decoration were introduced. In the lower lying areas of Bristol stucco facings appear to have been favoured up to the 1870's.

In a few streets of St. Philip's and along the Cheltenham and Gloucester Roads, High Victorian, barge-boarded and gable-ended terraces recall 16th and 17th century town house designs. But on the whole terracing between Lawrence Hill and Montpelier evolved from a debased 18th century form now built in brick, faced with stucco and decorated with coarse stone lintels. We know little about the builders who constructed them but the earlier buildings seem to reflect a feeling for Georgian proportions. We do know, however, that the architects, William Armstrong and Henry Rumley, both members of the Bristol Society of Architects did have large practices in the more sophisticated type of suburban planning.

Further expansion to the South covered the hillsides of Totterdown and parts of Bedminster with fine residential developments. From the 1850's onwards, winding terraces and crescents reflected the curves and outlines of the hills and, together with a wealth of discreet but inventive decoration, they still deserve our respect.

Until the later 19th century Clifton had enough land suitable for development to be able to continue to attract the most distinguished Victorian housing. The dramatic Georgian terraces were succeeded by far finer Regency and early Victorian ones on less spectacular sites. In Vyvyan Terrace of 1835, Richard Shackleton Pope gave prominence to a central pavilion through the introduction of an Ionic colonnade. But the articulation of the façade of the Royal Promenade on the north-west side of Victoria Square is infinitely more pleasing (see Plate 54), and, as its name implied, it is as much a palace as a terrace. The original design by Foster and Sons dates from 1837, though

PLATE 51

PLATE 50

Apsley Villas, a continuation of Kingsdown Parade,
Cotham, 1840   *Regional Buildings Record, University of Bath*

Semi-detached houses in College Road, Clifton, circa 1860
Regional Buildings Record, University of Bath

Albany Place, Montpelier, circa 1850
Partially demolished.   *Regional Buildings Record, University of Bath*

PLATE 52

Ashley Road, Montpelier, circa 1870
Partially demolished.   *Regional Buildings Record, University of Bath*

PLATE 53

PLATE 54

Royal Promenade, Victoria Square, Clifton
Foster and Sons, circa 1837.

Line engraving.

City Art Gallery, Bristol

Elmdale House, Clifton Down
George and Henry Godwin, circa 1867.
Built for Alderman Thomas Proctor
and presented by him to the
Corporation of Bristol for use as the
Mansion House in 1874.
The Builder, October 19th, 1867

PLATE 55

Claverton, Stoke Bishop
W. Wood Bethel, circa 1879.
The Building News, January 24th, 1879

PLATE 56

a decade or so passed before the terrace's completion. The small-scale arcade above the cornice, and the uninterrupted scrollwork of the pierced balustrade, horizontally unite the entire elevation in a way that departs from the 18th century treatment of terracing.

In the early 1850's Foster and Wood, as successors to James Foster, designed the south-west side of Victoria Square. Here there is elaborate Italianate arcading similar in its effect and close in date to Foster and Wood's shopping street in Queen's Road, which was once known as the Royal Parade. On its completion the Royal Parade was singled out as one of the few attempts to give architectural character and unity to both the ground and the upper storeys. Groups of three arches on the lower storey sprung from rusticated piers to mark the divisions between the shops and there were columns between the doors and windows. The attractive unified effect of this form of commercial terracing has been destroyed by modern shop fronts.

Worcester Terrace by Charles Underwood resembles the Royal Promenade in many ways. It was not completed until 1851–3, and by the 1860's a new type of detached or semi-detached house was to characterise the expansion of Clifton towards the Downs. These were generally of local red limestone excavated nearby or on site. Occasionally blue Pennant stone was used and Bath stone dressings, on which craftsmanlike decoration could be lavished, were universally applied.

A notable example was Elmdale House, built in 1867 by George and Henry Godwin for Alderman Thomas Proctor whose association with these architects was a close one (see Plate 55). In 1874 Proctor presented his house to the City as a Mansion House, and today it serves as such. We know that he wanted a functional style-less building with large well-lit rooms and an internal gallery. The entrance, unlike nearly all the other more pretentious mansions along the Promenade, faces Canynge Road, affording more shelter and a wide vista over the Downs from the huge bay windows.

As we have noticed, Charles Hansom's attempt to win gabled Gothic for Clifton had failed. It was the builders rather than the architects who were to so rapidly produce grand semi-detached houses and small villas in an Italianate style. Both Pembroke Road and College Road display houses of this type (see Plate 51). The use of well-defined quoins and string courses and of more costly stone was a luxurious variation of the high-density terracing in East Bristol. The builders employed in these schemes included George Gay, John Care and James Shorland.

In 1868 *The Builder* received an alarmed report that buildings in Clifton and Redland were being erected at such speed that they did not have the strength to stand up. Semi-detached villas in Clyde Road and Woolcott Park, were built out of the stone excavated on the site. The bow windows of attached houses were adjoined so closely to the party wall that there was not enough strength to support the wall above. The internal arrangement of the walls was so clumsy that with heavy blasting for adjacent sites, two homes collapsed. Some of the architects who did work in Clifton preferred to face their buildings in ashlar as was the case with William Henry Hawtin in Cambridge Park and James Adam Clark's detached houses in Victoria Square. But the predominant use of soft pink limestone and Bath stone in so many large houses, set in spacious and leafy surroundings, gives Redland and Clifton a pre-eminent position among English suburbs.

After the opening of the Clifton Suspension Bridge in 1864 elaborate mansions within small private estates began to appear in Leigh Woods, and these ranged in style from that of the Italian villa to the neo-Jacobean and the Scottish baronial. A Swiss chalet was probably an echo of another picturesque chalet of the 1840's which once stood on the

PLATE 57

Jacob's Wells Tenements, opposite Brandon Hill
Elijah Hoole, 1875.
Built for the Industrial Dwellings Company.   Demolished.

The Architect, August 21st, 1875

opposite bank of the Avon Gorge near to the Observatory.

By the 1870's and 1880's the areas which were to receive the most substantial Victorian houses were Sneyd Park and Stoke Bishop. W. Wood Bethell's house "Claverton", built in 1879 (see Plate 56), shows the advance in taste which had occurred since the early years of the Clifton development. The pretensions to grandeur were self-consciously modelled on the irregular planning and craft-like principles of late medieval houses. A new form of architecture had permeated Gothic Revival housing. Bay windows and high-pitched roofs were used but with no feeling for the true Gothic style. Here the transomed windows are square-headed and the pretty oriels and galleries are disposed for a pleasing visual effect. Facade architecture in domestic buildings of this scale no longer existed; asymmetry had taken its place. There are multitudinous variations in the outer suburbs of Bristol of this type of house which, on a more modest scale, continued to be built up to the Second World War. The 1870's also satisfied the need for small scale villas and such planned developments took shape in Alexandra Park, Cotham, where each street name honours Sir Walter Scott. Extensive gap-filling between the streets of large-scale houses of the preceding decade was to take place throughout Clifton, Redland and Henleaze.

Rapid urban expansion during the 19th century had brought the hardships of overcrowding. With the passing of the Public Health Act in 1872, Urban Sanitary Authorities were created throughout the country. The work of Medical Officers of Health, Sanitary Inspectors and Surveyors began to alleviate the distressing social conditions of slum life.

Public interest in the poor conditions of city housing had been aroused by the Bristol press. Through the Housing of the Working Classes Act of 1890 the Council appointed an Artisan Dwellings Committee and later a Housing of the Working Classes Committee which undertook the repair of unfit houses and the provision of accommodation for families displaced because of demolition. The Council did not provide for or subsidise housing until the passing of the Housing Act in 1919.

However, voluntary philanthropic organisations had earlier made attempts to provide decent housing. A movement was started by Susannah Winkworth who had hired two or three large houses in Dowry Square and let them to poor families at low rentals. The success of the project prompted the foundation of the Industrial Dwellings Company in 1874 with a capital of £20,000. A lease was obtained from the Merchant Venturers' Society for a plot of land at Jacob's Wells near Brandon Hill. Here three blocks of tenements forming an open-ended quadrangle were constructed to designs by the London architect, Elijah Hoole (see Plate 57). Each block possessed broad stone staircases and galleries with balustrades, onto which the room doors opened. Sculleries, cupboards, range ovens and communal dust shutes were provided. Water was laid on at each landing and gas provided on the stairs and balconies but not in the rooms. The buildings presented a castellated appearance in what was then becoming a rather outmoded Gothic institutional style.

LATER VICTORIAN BUILDINGS

The departure of Godwin in 1865 had signalled a decline in the Bristol Architectural and Archaeological Society, as it was then styled. A perfunctory record of the Society's activities up to 1867 exists and thereafter there is an absence of information for the succeeding two decades. Hectic building activity continued apace, but no local stylistic coherence or creative element, comparable to that of the sixties, is identifiable. The discipline of the Gothic Revival had never made any real impression on Bristol's architecture. In the hands of a few talented men such as Gingell, Godwin, Foster and Ponton an adventurous interpretation of medieval forms had been formulated. But in Bristol that inspiration was to be later dissipated in the face of a profusion of revived styles.

Nevertheless, much of Bristol's architecture built from 1870 could still be remarkably inventive in the use of local materials of which there was a rich and varied supply, in both brick and stone. Eccentricities, too, can delight us; Stuart Colman's disposition, in 1874, of the daintiest lancets on the patterned red brick facade to the Museum Lecture Theatre in University Road is charming. So also is the exotic decoration of the former Bazaar and Winter Gardens, of 1878, in Boyce's Avenue in Clifton. This building, which is now a warehouse, contained a gallery and a rose window of extravagant proportions. It was the work of the builder, Joseph William King, who is credited with an imaginative scheme to construct an enormous viaduct from the heights of Perry Road across to Small Street in the business centre of the City.

In large-scale public or institutional buildings, in which some associative style was required, we find that, where a Gothic style is chosen, the convinced vigour of the earlier Revival buildings is lacking. In 1877 Foster and Wood were requested to draw up plans for new premises for the Bristol Grammar School. The Headmaster, the Reverend J. W. Caldicott, was born in Birmingham and educated at the King Edward VI Grammar School, an important early Gothic building of 1834–7 by Sir Charles Barry. One can presume it was Caldicott's expressed wish that the new buildings should follow the Grammar School tradition, to which the Perpendicular Great Hall certainly conforms. Pink rubble and Bath stone dressings were used on a vast and impressive scale, but the architects were allowed no imaginative display.

Nearby, Charles Francis Hansom's buildings for the young University College founded in 1876, though still in a Gothic style, reveal a departure from the Puginesque coherence of design which Hansom had demonstrated in Clifton College. The Medical School buildings required more spacious planning and better lighting than traceried windows could allow. Therefore the practical two-stage plan was chosen from the competition to which Stuart Colman had unsuccessfully submitted a fabulous but heavy-going Gothic design. An illustration of Hansom's projected building accompanied a note in *The Architect* (see Plate 58), which commented on Hansom's resistance to the aberrations of the pretentious "Queen Anne" style which was currently gaining favour. The buildings were constructed from 1880 onwards.

Hansom was also to enter a competition for the new Merchant Venturers' Technical College formed from the Trade and Mining School then in Nelson Street, which was one of the earliest science schools in the country. But in this case, his smartly printed prospectus was overlooked in favour of a manuscript one by Edward Cookworthy Robins, a Londoner, who had demonstrated his ability to

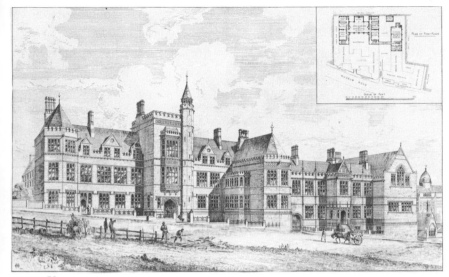

PLATE 58

University College, University Road
Charles Francis Hansom, 1880–3.
Published design and plan for the proposed Medical School and future buildings. The present buildings which belong to the University of Bristol do not conform exactly to this design, but the same elements occur.
The Architect, May 10th, 1879

Colston's Girls' Day School, Cheltenham Road
William Venn Gough, 1891.

PLATE 59

City Museum, Bristol

Cabot Tower, Brandon Hill
William Venn Gough, 1897–8.
Photograph circa 1900.

PLATE 60

City Museum, Bristol

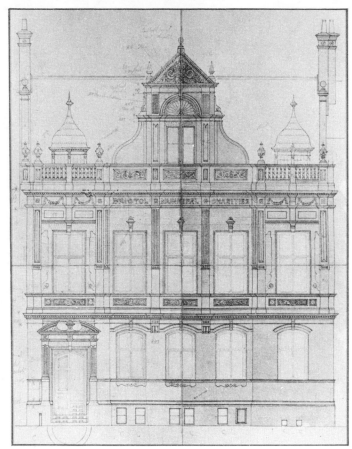

PLATE 61

The former offices of the Bristol Municipal Charities, Colston Avenue
John Foster and Joseph Wood, 1884.
Original pen and ink and wash design.
The building is now called Quay Head House.   *Bristol Municipal Charities*

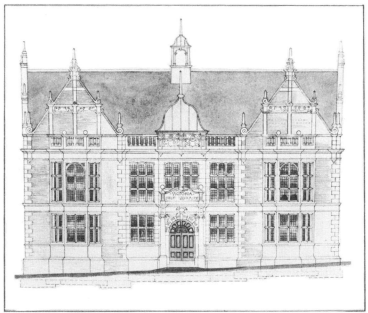

PLATE 62

The Victoria Free Library, St. George's Park
Frank William Wills, 1898.
Original pen and ink and wash design.
Angus Meek Russell Diplock Associates

design a modern, functional building which would compare with the more advanced continental schools. The heating and ventilating systems which he applied were indeed sophisticated, as were the type of furnaces, flues and drains in the laboratories. Robins was a specialist architect and wrote a book, *Technical School and College Building*, in 1887, in which he emphasised the importance of laboratory practice in this form of education.

The new L-shaped building in Unity Street was opened in 1885 and serves today as a Polytechnic college. It is of a modified Gothic design, but block-like in form and four storeyed in elevation. Local materials such as hard blue Pennant stone and the usual Bath stone dressings were used and were combined with the Cattybrook Company's deep red brick. A powerful use of the same brick within a Gothic elevation appeared in Sir Frank Will's East Street tobacco factory of W. D. & H. O. Wills in 1888; today the building forms a beautiful piece of street architecture.

Cattybrook bricks had formed the Burgundian patterning of Foster's Almshouses by Foster and Wood and had given the Granary its striking character. They were extensively used in all types of buildings throughout Bristol. The Cattybrook Works at Almondsbury were founded in 1865 by Charles Richardson, the engineer of the Bristol and South Wales Union Railway. During the excavation of the Patchway Tunnel he had noticed that the clay would produce high quality engineering bricks. When, in 1872, the Great Western Railway Company adopted a plan for the construction of a tunnel under the Severn, Richardson, as Chief Engineer, used some thirty million bricks from his own works for the lining of the tunnel. Not only red, but buff, blue and yellow bricks were issued by this firm. The combination of red and yellow, in an admittedly begrimed state, can still be observed in such buildings as those by the Fish Market in Baldwin Street or in the former half-destroyed Lewin's Mead Brewery by William Bruce Gingell. By the turn of the century the new factories built for the major industrial firms in Bristol all showed some

sharp-edged addition built in rich Cattybrook brick.

Frederick Bligh Bond became the partner of Charles Francis Hansom in 1886 and together they continued work on the University buildings, and on the provision of new schools for the School Board which had been established in 1871. Bond was associated with the larger schools at Easton Road, Ashton Gate and Barley Fields. In general the building style of Bristol's Board schools is academic and restrained.

Early in his career William Venn Gough had trained under Hansom; his association with Archibald Ponton has already been mentioned in connection with the Church of the Holy Nativity at Knowle and the Granary. He was one of the first young Bristol architects to pass the examination for admission to the Royal Institute of British Architects. He started practice on his own in 1878. In such buildings as the Colston Girls' Day School, Cheltenham Road (see Plate 59), Gough appeared to be caught between a bewildering variety of styles. The quattro-cento windows are set against Northern Renaissance gables and, in plan, it is attempting to resemble a Jacobean mansion. A similar mood of confusion appears in the Trinity Road Library. The profusion of little embellishments in the form of volutes, pediments and finials has no meaning. One of his more successful works, the former Port of Bristol Authority offices in Queen Square of 1899, shows a more sophisticated treatment of the facade and the chimneys relate well to the high-pitched roof. But it was as though the opportunity to build in the largest and most distinguished square in Bristol went to his head; the building shows little sensitivity towards its Georgian and Regency neighbours.

Gough's moment of potential triumph came in 1898 with the opening of the Cabot Tower on Brandon Hill (see Plate 60). The previous year had marked the fourth centenary of the discovery of the mainland of North America by John and Sebastian Cabot, who had set sail from Bristol. The lavish ceremonial which surrounded the laying of the foundation stone on the centenary day, 24th June, was matched by celebrations organised by the Royal Society of Canada at Halifax in Nova Scotia. The memorial tower is one hundred and five feet high and set on the most conspicuous site in Bristol. The apex of the fanciful Gothic decoration on the upper storey is surmounted by a gilded and winged figure representing commerce mounted on a globe symbolising the world.

In spite of Gough's scholarly pretensions, his independent work was somewhat brash. The old established firm of Foster and Wood could show a more graceful departure from their former Gothic or Byzantine idioms. As architects to the trustees of the Bristol Municipal Charities they were required to build offices for that body in 1884 (see Plate 61).

By this date taste in office and commercial design had moved away from both Gothic and Italianate forms. The London architects, Philip Webb, Norman Shaw and Eden Nesfield promoted the adoption of unadorned brick facades and tall bay windows, which, in street architecture, provided improved lighting. The Dutch brickwork and white windows of Shaw's New Zealand Chambers built in 1873 in the City of London, provided the formula on which the more advanced architects were to base their designs. The high Victorian Venetian or Classical palaces of finance were now an anachronism and the romantic historical associations which these buildings once evoked were now overtaken by a desire for the more realistic domesticity of the small business house.

In Bristol the new idea of the Domestic Revival office was to penetrate more slowly. If we return now to study the old Bristol Municipal Charities Building on Colston Avenue, we can notice the intimations of change. It is a free classical building with a northern Renaissance pedimented gable and elegant dressings in stone applied to a plain brick wall. The flat pilasters, neat balustrades with urns and a William and Mary doorway are luxurious but not overbearing and there is discreet detailing in the brickwork. The interior of the building contains an elaborately carved wooden stair-well and much dark wood panelling and stained glass. This attention to detail is characteristic of the firm of Foster and Wood; the beautiful traceried oak galleries and porches of Trinity and Foster's almshouses and the fanciful Gothic iron-work in the form of railings and lanterns showed just the same care and devotion.

If we turn our attention to some of the better libraries and schools such as those built by Frank William Wills, the author of the previously mentioned factory in Bedminster, we find the same domestic spirit of the 17th century in a building such as the Victoria Free Library, St. George Park, of 1898 (see Plate 62). Here the interpretation follows a neo-Jacobean style with a decorative use of the quoins, a small curvilinear cupola and paned-glass windows. Even the ground plan is E-shaped in the Jacobean manner. Frank Wills succeeded Foster and Wood as architect to the Trustees of the Muncipal Charities and achieved an immaculate domestic style in such brick buildings as the new Red Maids School in Westbury Road, 1911.

For a more prestigious building such as the City Art Gallery, in Queen's Road, Wills produced a free Baroque design of magnificent proportions. Here, as in the case of earlier 19th century buildings, such as the nearby Royal West of England Academy, a Beaux-Arts sculpture group forms the crowning feature. This building was constructed between 1899 and 1904 and exemplifies the Edwardian-Imperial-Baroque style which architects, Norman Shaw included, turned to when a grand opulent effect seemed suitable for such public buildings as libraries, town halls and hotels. But the pleasing homeliness of St. George's Library is just as an important facet of Wills' style and equally appropriate to the age. He took a special interest in the improved construction of farm buildings and even designed a cricket pavilion.

The thoroughfare of Baldwin Street was redeveloped in

PLATE 63

The People's Palace, Baldwin Street
James Hutton. Opened 1892.
This building exists today as the Gaumont Cinema but the upper storey has been refaced and the glass canopy removed.
Early 20th century photograph.
Avon County Library

E-Shed, Dean's Marsh, facing St. Augustine's Parade
Edward Gabriel's pen and ink and watercolour design for a dockside shed and entry gates submitted successfully to a competition held by the Corporation's Docks Committee in 1894.
The Port of Bristol Authority

PLATE 64

63

PLATE 66

The former Prudential Assurance Company Building, Clare Street
Alfred Waterhouse, 1899.
Copy of the original pen and ink design.

The Prudential Assurance Company Limited

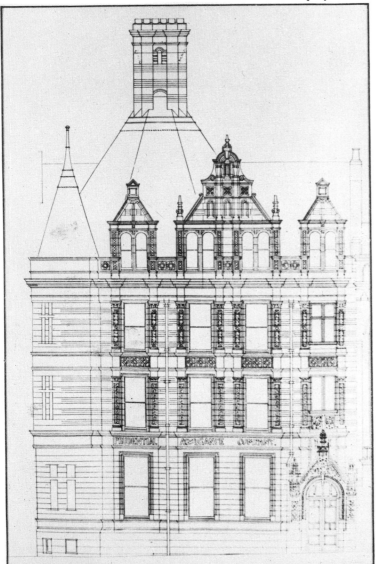

PLATE 65

Facade of the former Edward Everard Printing Works and Offices, Broad Street
In 1900 Henry Williams designed the works which extended from Broad Street through to Little John Street. The spectacular appearance of the facade should be credited to W. J. Neatby of the firm of Doulton and Company who devised the ceramic decoration. The building now forms part of an office complex of the National Westminster Bank; the facade has been preserved.

Regional Buildings Record, University of Bath

1874 and involved the demolition of many ancient town houses. The widening began at the Bristol Bridge end and finished with John Bevan's French-styled Dunlop and Mackie premises which turned the corner into Broad Quay. From the 1880's the street filled up with modest brick-fronted office blocks and bank and insurance buildings which increasingly displayed simple free classical facades. Undistinguished and slight as many of them were, they have now acquired a look of vulnerable preciosity in the face of 20th century development.

Along with this later phase of commercial building came the new buildings for public entertainment. One of the principal Victorian theatres was the now demolished Prince's Theatre in Park Row by the Bath architect, Charles John Phipps (1835-97), who designed the Savoy, the Lyric and Her Majesty's Theatre in London. It was the Prince's Theatre rather than Bristol's Theatre Royal which then provided serious drama.

The popular enthusiasm for Music Hall entertainment had prompted the Livermore Brothers, who had an almost national monopoly in this field, to employ James Hutton to design the People's Palace on Baldwin Street (see Plate 63). When it opened in 1892 it held three thousand people and was one of the first places of entertainment to be lit by electricity. This building exists today as the Gaumont Cinema, although the proud brick lettering has been faced over. The following year the Empire in Old Market Street opened, and for this theatre, the architects, Wylson and Long, produced a fanciful Moorish design. Picture theatres sometimes called Electric Theatres and skating rinks, proliferated in the 1900's.

By the 1890's several of the major local architects of the mid-Victorian period had ceased to practise and the work of the surviving elder members of the profession had lost its former authority.

There are no records from 1867 to 1889 of the Bristol Architectural and Archaeological Society which Godwin had re-styled from the original Bristol Society of Architects. Thereafter there are intermittent reports which indicate that some attempt to revitalise the professional Society had been made in 1888. But the effective rebirth of the Society occurred only in 1914 from which date a continuous record of its activities was kept. Moves towards the formal education of student members culminated in 1921 when a school of architecture was founded.

The younger generation of architects working in Bristol during the 1880's and 1890's was composed of men who had been articled to the early founding members of the Bristol Society of Architects, but they were now to be joined by outsiders. In the absence of any professional unity during the 1870's and 1880's a disparate form of architecture comparable with that of other major provincial centres emerged. The local stylistic cohesion of the heroic decade of the 1860's could not easily be recaptured. Specialisation and the opportunity of receiving technical instruction outside Bristol prompted these younger architects to be more conscious of national trends. Both local and visiting architects were now to give Bristol a few very interesting late Victorian buildings.

Edward Gabriel, son of the Bristol architect, Samuel Burleigh Gabriel, built a number of schools and hotels during the 1890's and 1900's. The most prominent example of his work which survives today is the dock building, known as E Shed (see Plate 64). The Port authorities considered that a shed which stood by the Floating Harbour facing St. Augustine's Parade, should be embellished with an end facade so that the shed roof would not show above the gable. The authorities also required that the building should have an attractive aspect from College Green. Gabriel's design won the competition in 1894. It incorporated a florid sculpture-filled pediment and a strategically placed polygonal tower surmounted by a curved dome. Norman Shaw had used strong horizontal bands and circular corner turrets and domes in his design for the New Scotland

Yard Building in 1887. But at E Shed Gabriel, like Gingell in his General Hospital and in his former E. S. and A. Robinson Building, used corner towers and domes as important structural features. In a hilly, haphazardly planned city like Bristol, the oblique view was all important and there were few places in the old part of the city where grand symmetrically planned facades could be set off to full advantage.

In 1897 a commentary on recent architectural developments in Bristol was published in *The Builder*. The writer stressed the enhancement of the city's picturesque qualities by the presence of shipping along its many waterfronts. He singled out for praise some of the more important buildings of the mid-Victorian period, but turned his back on the new and "good but unimpressive" works in the city centre and found himself lost in admiration for Prince Street by the Harbour which held so many curious associations of social, commercial and architectural change.

The observations of this commentator confirmed that the most impressive and coherent architectural schemes of Victorian Bristol had belonged to the 1860's and early 1870's but we must remember that, at the time of his writing, several important buildings were still about to be erected.

In Clare Street we find a beautiful deep red terracotta building on the corner of St. Stephen's Avenue (see Plate 65). It was the work of the prominent architect, Alfred Waterhouse (1830–1905), one of whose earlier works was the large Gothic Town Hall at Manchester, 1869–77. He retained a Gothic style for the headquarters of the Prudential Assurance Company in Holborn, begun in 1876. That building is gabled with lancet windows and has a large central tower. But the character of the building is determined by the unusual use of sharp, red, imperishable terracotta brick. As architect to the Prudential, Waterhouse was asked to design a branch office in Bristol in 1899. Here again red terracotta is applied but, this time, to a building in

the style of the Loire Palaces. Full advantage is taken of its corner site by placing round pinnacled turrets at two corners of the building and a polygonal central roof is surmounted by a massive chimney stack. The decorative skyline is unlike that of any other building in the area. The use of pre-moulded terracotta brick gives a rigid almost synthetic form of decoration and it is neatly applied here on pilasters and around the balustrades and entrance. However the total effect is sharp, stylish and obviously the work of a metropolitan architect.

A local architect, Henry Williams, used terracotta brick very effectively on the sides and rear of the former Edward Everard's printing works, Broad Street, which is more familiarly known to us by its famous multi-coloured tiled facade, built in 1900 (see Plate 66). Only a small portion of the body of the building remains today in John Street and it is now incorporated, together with the facade, into a modern complex of the National Westminster Bank. The lower storey of the sides was arcuated in the Bristol fashion and was surmounted by a smaller castellated and turreted block. In the surviving fragment we can still enjoy the spirited use of pre-moulded terracotta; a dragon clings fiercely to a drain-head. Such dragons were once in pairs. Many such decorative devices were produced in terracotta by the firm of Barham Brothers of Bridgwater.

This was modern architecture, mass produced and disdainful of traditional methods of craftsmanship. It was cheaper than stonework, more accurate in repetition and less perishable. But the glorious facade of the printing works, is also a symbol of the craft revival.

Everard, the owner of the printing works, was determined that his building should be a memorial to the masters of his craft. In 1902 he published, *A Bristol Printing House*, which explained how the idea of the facade had evolved. Gutenburg had instigated a new era in printing and William Morris had revived the art in the mid-19th century. Both men are featured in the facade and between them is a

PLATE 67

The Convent of the Sisters of Charity, Redcatch Road, Knowle
John Dando Sedding, 1890–1.
Various features in the present building depart from this published design. The Chapel of a different design by G. F. Bodley was built in 1900 at the rear of the building and the sculptural embellishments are lacking. The laundry can be seen to the right. The Convent is now known as the St. Agnes Retreat House.
The Builder, June 14th, 1890

winged figure representing the Spirit of Literature; in the gable above a symbol of Light and Truth appears. Everard's interest in medieval art led to an investigation of Byzantine and Celtic forms, and he drew himself a rough plan of such a facade with grotesque animal friezes. He then collaborated with W. J. Neatby of the ceramic firm of Doulton and Company, and Neatby proposed the scheme of decoration in the new Carrara marble-ware tiles. Neatby was the firm's designer of polychrome tiles for architectural use and as a result of his experiments he produced glazed tiles which could be used for external decoration without deterioration from the effects of weather. He designed and printed the tiles himself. The architectural design is loosely Byzantine in form, although Everard wished the lower storey to conform to the triple archway of the nearby Church of St. John on Bristol's medieval wall. The result was an exceptional one; for Neatby it was triumph in the reconciliation of art and industry in the best spirit of the 19th century craft revival, and for Everard it represented the fulfilment of a personal and commercial ambition.

Of great importance to the future of 20th century architecture was the Domestic Revival, which, as we have seen, took its inspiration from the works of Norman Shaw and Eden Nesfield. The so called "Queen Anne" style had appeared from the 1880's onwards in the form of office buildings and fashionable London residences. But the architects who had created a modern style from 17th and 18th century architecture, had, at an earlier stage, turned to medieval vernacular architecture for new inspiration. William Morris, Philip Webb, Norman Shaw and, here we introduce John Dando Sedding (1837–91), had all trained in the office of George Edmund Street, the academic Gothic architect whose work in Bristol we have already described. The young group of architects respected Street's craftsmanship, and they inherited his enthusiasm for iron work, good masonry in local materials, joinery, and even needlework. But they developed their own styles and Webb and Shaw were to become the founders of a new type of modern housing.

John Dando Sedding left Street's office in 1865 and moved to Bristol in 1868 to become Precentor of St. Raphael's mission, which has been mentioned in connection with Woodyer's Chapel and Almshouses. He studied Somerset's medieval buildings during his stay in Bristol, but, with little architectural patronage, he returned to London in 1875. It was not until 1890, a year before his death, that Bristol could enjoy a major work by this important architect.

The Order of the Sisters of Charity, founded in 1869, had occupied a building along the Cumberland Road adjacent to St. Raphael's Chapel and by the 1890's the Order required a new House of Charity to accommodate the community of nuns and the children in their care. Sedding was called upon to design what was alternatively called an Industrial School at Redcatch Road in Knowle. The Sisters of Charity occupy this building today. It does not conform exactly to the published illustration (see Plate 67). The disposition of the bays was altered and a chapel was built in 1900 at the rear of the building to advanced designs of great simplicity by George Frederick Bodley.

Unlike any other building in Bristol at that time, it revealed the new feeling for vernacular medieval architecture, although some 17th century styled oriel windows do appear. Shaw and Nesfield had already experimented with the use of massive gables and timber framing, and Sedding, in touch with such developments, employed them here. A striking part of the design was the laundry, still used as such. It can be seen to the right. The interior displays a great delight in the use of traditional features such as the floral patterned plaster work in the ceilings, wide inglenooks and stone passages.

At the turn of the century the local architect, Henry Dare Bryan, was to employ the Domestic Revival style which, by then, had been widely publicised through illustrations in the architectural journals. He set up practice in 1890 and built various restaurants and offices in the city. Handsome houses at Downleaze in Sneyd Park show a mixture of the

**Bristol Central Library,
Deanery Road**
Charles Holden, 1906.
The eastern elevation facing
College Square.
Pen and ink drawing
by Samuel J. Loxton
Avon County Library

PLATE 68

PLATE 69

**The former
Western Congregational College,
Cotham Road**
Henry Dare Bryan, 1905–6.
Pen and ink drawing
by Samuel J. Loxton.
Avon County Library

old Victorian elements with some novel features, but the White House in Leigh Woods, built in 1901, reveals a full understanding of the new style. It has a deep pitched roof, coupled gables and quaint shutters.

More substantial is the former Western Congregational College on Cotham Road, built in 1905 (see Plate 69). Early designs for this building adopt the same angle plan, but were in an elaborate Edwardian classical mode. These were rejected in favour of ones in a more imposing but comfortable Jacobean style.

There are some Tudor features in the Deanery Road facade of the Bristol Central Library. But it is not eclectic in character, and it is impossible to classify it by the use of historical terms. The building was constructed in 1906 by a partnership of London architects, Percy Adams, Charles Holden and Lionel Pearson. Holden (1875–1960), who was the acknowledged designer of the group, had trained under C. R. Ashbee (1863–1942), and he was destined to become one of the most distinguished architects of the inter-war years, designing the London Transport headquarters at St. James's and a number of tube stations. In the Library, Holden reconciled the practical requirements of a modern library with an architectural recognition of a Norman gateway with a restored Tudor superstructure to which the Library was actually attached. The recessed oriels and shallow gables are suitably discreet as are the semi-circular bays containing sculpture groups by Sir Charles Pibworth. Holden considered sculpture to be an integral part of architecture; for his British Medical Association Building on the Strand, 1907–08, Sir Jacob Epstein was the chosen sculptor.

But the east side of the Library (see Plate 68), exhibits a freedom and boldness which must certainly derive from the work of the Art Nouveau architect, Charles Rennie Mackintosh (1868–1928), whose best known work is the Glasgow School of Art, begun in 1896. The library wing of that building possesses a robust character comparable to that of Bristol's Library and was constructed in 1907–09.

In 1906 the same firm designed a new building for the Bristol Royal Infirmary on Upper Maudlin Street. It was on a prominent hillside site and the whiteness of the Portland stone was unusual to Bristol. The building is simple and blocklike in form and almost devoid of external decoration. Within a few decades this building was to be considered one of the first examples in the country of a building which relied for its effect on mass and proportion alone.

In the years preceding the outbreak of the First World War, building continued apace. As we have seen, local architects, such as E. Gabriel, H. Dare Bryan, E. H. Edwards and F. W. Wills, could exhibit a mastery of current styles. Even the now conventional firm of Foster and Wood, could, in 1904, insert in St. Stephen's Street, off Colston Avenue, a stylish Arts and Crafts building, once the offices of the *Bristol Times and Mirror*.

In the field of ecclesiastical architecture it must be admitted that few advances had been made since the 1870's. The exception is provided by the visiting architect, George Frederick Bodley (1837–1907), whose work can be seen in the chapel at the Convent of the Sisters of Charity at Knowle, and in the small church of St. Aidan at Nag's Head Hill in St. George. Both were built between 1901 and 1904, and reveal on a small scale his fastidiously simple and modern adaptation of the Gothic style.

Our admiration of the very progressive work of Sedding and Holden should not convey the impression that, as in the years preceding Victoria's reign, the best architecture in Bristol was the work of outside architects. But there is nothing in the record of Bristol's 19th century architecture to prepare for the ultimate monument to the Victorian era, the University tower by Sir George Oatley.

George Oatley (1863–1950), will be remembered as one of

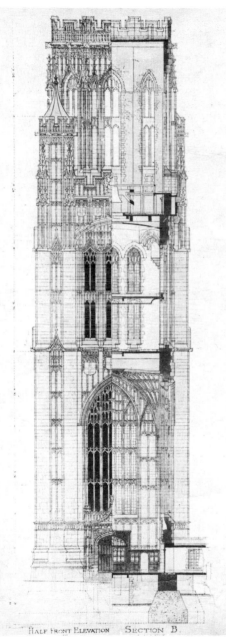

The University of Bristol, Wills Memorial Building, Queen's Road
George Herbert Oatley and George Churchus Lawrence, 1914–25.
Copies of the original pen and ink and wash designs of 1914. Half front elevation and half section of the tower. Part elevation of the tower and section of the entrance chamber, stairs and vestibule.

The University of Bristol

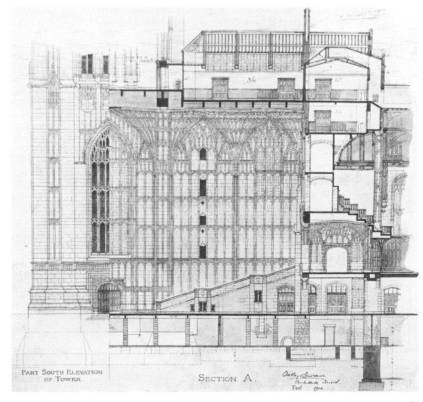

PLATE 70

71

the greatest local architects, whose energetic devotion to the Gothic style was equal to that of some of his most prominent Victorian forbears.

Oatley received his architectural training on the Isle of Wight in the office of Thomas Dashwood, and began his career in Bristol in 1879 as assistant to Henry Crisp. He became Crisp's partner in 1888, and, until Crisp's death in 1896, they carried out a variety of institutional and ecclesiastical works of a minor sort. But in 1899 at The Church of All Hallows, Easton, Oatley had an opportunity of exercising his ability to employ an academically informed Gothic style. Its tall interior, transepts and ambulatory revealed a sensitive study of French Gothic of the 14th century. Although the church is incomplete, its scale is impressive, and there is an obvious power and originality in the design which overlooks the contemporary niceties of the Domestic Revival.

In partnership with another local architect, George Churchus Lawrence, who was to devote much of his energy to the revitalisation of the Bristol Society of Architects, Oatley divided his attention between commercial buildings in the current Neo-Georgian style of the 1900's and the vast project of creating a new academic centre for the University of Bristol.

In a letter to the Council of the University, Sir George Arthur Wills and Henry Herbert Wills, sons of the first Chancellor of the University, the third Henry Overton Wills, stated that the dignity of the University, which had received its charter in 1909, should now be enhanced by new additions. They considered that the existing buildings were not sufficiently outstanding. In 1912 they accordingly offered to finance the construction of a building to the memory of their father.

Land on the site of the demolished Blind Asylum at the top of Park Street offered a suitable location for a building which would present its elevation to the main thorough-fare of Queen's Road. The Wills brothers had already consulted Oatley and his preliminary designs for buildings and a tower, in an appropriately collegiate late Gothic style, were approved (see Plate 70). Work began on the eve of the First World War, was resumed after the Armistice and finally completed in 1925; George V performed the opening ceremony in June of that year.

The building contained lecture rooms, offices, libraries, a Great Hall bearing an oak hammer-beamed roof, a fan-vaulted vestibule and entrance chamber, and a polygonal Council Chamber. The scale and virtuosity of the designs for the entire complex proved that the Gothic style with all its traditional dressings could still provide immense freedom to an architect with such flair and courage. Oatley's command of the style enabled him to take refreshing liberties with complete success and in doing so produced a work of modern rather than revived Gothic.

The masons, joiners and plasterers were allowed great flexibility; the carving was Gothic but the cut was modern. Sculptured heads were incorporated, but not in the form of archaeological copies. They even included a tin-helmeted soldier and a bearded professor.

The tower itself, built of Bath and Clipsham stone, is a masterpiece, monumental in scale and the dominating landmark of the city. The decorative ogee-arched decoration of the preliminary design was abandoned in favour of one of a more severe effect around the lower storeys, the ornamental tracery being reserved for the uppermost section of the octagonal lantern.

Oatley's plans and designs for the building are now held by the University itself. Amongst them is a very rough sketch design on a small sheet of paper. Here the towers of Fountains Abbey and those of the Cathedrals of Bristol and Gloucester are sketched, measured and drawn alongside a design for the University tower which in height exceeds them all.

BIBLIOGRAPHICAL NOTE

In June 1950, Lance Wright, the present Editor of the *Architectural Review*, published "An Account of the Bristol Society of Architects, 1850–1950" in the Centenary Number of the *Journal of the Bristol and Somerset Society of Architects*. This article represents the first scholarly study of Victorian architecture in Bristol. In the same year an exhibition of photographs of Bristol's Victorian buildings was also organised by Lance Wright and held in the City Art Gallery, Bristol. The exhibition text and the above mentioned article laid a foundation upon which I have relied heavily.

In June 1968, the Victorian Society published both detailed typescript notes by David Lloyd on the architecture of Bristol and its outer districts, and a commentary by Patrick Brown on the industrial and commercial architecture of Victorian Bristol.

The following reference books are indispensable to a study of Victorian buildings in Bristol and contain accounts of 19th century architectural developments:

John Latimer, *The Annals of Bristol in the 19th century*, Bristol, Vol. VI, 1887; Vol. VII, 1902.

Bristol in 1898–99 and Contemporary Biographies, two volumes published by W. T. Pike and Co., Brighton, 1899.

Tudor Edwards, *Bristol*, London, 1951.

Bryan Little, *The City and County of Bristol*, Birmingham and London, 1954.

Sir Nikolaus Pevsner, *The Buildings of England: North Somerset and Bristol*, Harmondsworth, 1958.

Reece Winstone, *Bristol's Earliest Photographs*, Bristol, 1970, one of twenty volumes in the *Bristol As It Was* series, 1960–74, in which Bristol's Victorian buildings are listed, dated and attributed.

Angus Buchanan and Neil Cossons, *Industrial History in Pictures: Bristol*, Newton Abbot, 1970.

T. H. B. Burrough, *City Building Series: Bristol*, London, 1970.

Dorothy Brown, *Bristol and How it Grew*, Bristol, 1974.

Some standard works of reference on Victorian architecture are:

Henry Russell Hitchcock, *Early Victorian Architecture in Britain* (two volumes), London and New Haven, 1954.

Robert Furneaux Jordan, *Victorian Architecture*, Harmondsworth, 1966.

Volumes in the *Royal Institute of British Architects Drawings Series*, General Editor, John Harris, provide concise introductions to special aspects of architecture and contain useful bibliographies. Relevant to 19th century studies are the volumes: *The Greek Revival* by J. Mordaunt Crook; *Victorian Churches* by P. Howell, and *Monuments to Commerce* by N. Taylor, all three published in 1968.

ACKNOWLEDGEMENTS

My sincere thanks are due to the many representatives of firms, institutions, schools and churches throughout Bristol who have generously given me information, allowed me access to their buildings and records, and who have kindly permitted the reproduction of drawings and photographs in their possession. The sources of the illustrations are indicated in the captions. Mrs. Jane Fawcett, the Secretary of the Victorian Society, very kindly permitted me to study notes on the restoration of Bristol Cathedral which will be incorporated into her book, *The Changing Fabric of English Cathedrals*. Mr. Paul R. Joyce has also provided me with extensive notes on the work of G. E. Street in Bristol. I would like to thank the many architects in Bristol who have helped me in my research, and who have allowed me to study their firms' records and drawings. I am particularly grateful to Mr. Eustace Button, Mr. Hugh Ingram, Mr. Alan Rome, and to Mr. Michael Biggs, Secretary of the Avon Branch of the R.I.B.A., the Bristol Society of Architects.

I am very much indebted to the members of staff of the following organisations for all their assistance and advice: The Avon County Library; The Bristol Record Office; The Regional Buildings Record, Bath University; The Port of Bristol Authority; The City Estates Department, Bristol Corporation; The University of Bristol; the Bristol Municipal Charities; the Department of Prints and Drawings of the Victoria and Albert Museum; The Royal Institute of British Architects, Drawings Collection and the National Monuments Record. Mr. Derek Balmer and Mr. William Colyer undertook much of the photography.

My colleagues in the City Museum and Art Gallery have assisted me in many ways, but I am specially grateful to Mr. Francis Greenacre, the Curator of Fine Art, for all his guidance, advice and help in my preparations for this booklet.

INDEX

Numbers in bold type are page numbers of illustrations. Only references to local buildings and streets, etc., are included. Individual owners' names, patrons, etc., are not included.

CHURCHES, CHAPELS, etc.

BUILDINGS except Churches, Chapels, etc.

Wills, W. D. and H. O., offices, Redcliffe Street, Foster and Wood, **46, 48**
Wool Hall, St. Thomas's Street, R. S. Pope, 41
Worcester Terrace, Clifton, Underwood, 55

STREETS